SALES PROMOTION AND
MODERN MERCHANDISING

PERSPECTIVES IN MARKETING SERIES
Robert D. Buzzell and Frank M. Bass, Consulting Editors

SALES PROMOTION AND MODERN MERCHANDISING

John F. Luick
Vice President
Luick & Watrous, Inc.

William Lee Ziegler
Assistant Professor of Marketing
School of Business Administration
Seton Hall University

McGraw-Hill Book Company
New York
St. Louis
San Francisco
Toronto
London
Sydney

for Elizabeth and Rita

EDITORS' PREFACE

This book is the seventh to appear in the *Perspectives in Marketing* series. Like its predecessors, it is designed to provide a more intensive treatment of a marketing topic than is normally given by basic textbooks in the field.

Sales promotion is not, of course, a new development in marketing. On the contrary, it is as old as organized economic exchange. Along with personal selling and advertising, sales promotion is one of the basic tools of persuasion used to facilitate and consummate transactions. Unlike personal selling and advertising, however, sales promotion has received relatively little attention from marketing scholars or from researchers in industry. As a result, there have been no systematic guides available to the marketing student or practitioner. Yet sales promotion is a sufficiently important tool of marketing—and a sufficiently large component of total marketing cost—to warrant careful study.

The importance of sales promotion is reflected both in the substantial amounts spent on it by business and in the controversies surrounding some kinds of promotion. Total expenditures on promotion in the United States amount to some $4 billion per year, or about one-fourth as much as total advertising expenditure. The effects of these expenditures are just as uncertain as those of advertising, and the potential for improvement is no doubt correspondingly great.

During the 1950s and 1960s, several forms of sales promotion came under attack by government agencies and consumer groups. Trading stamps and supermarket "games," in particular, were widely criticized as tending to increase consumer prices and to encourage excessive market control at the retail level. Intelligent discussion of these issues was severely limited by lack of basic facts about sales promotion, its costs, and its role in the marketing system.

We hope that this book will help to remedy the lack of authoritative sources on sales promotion, and that its publication will stimulate further investigation and appraisal of this important element of modern marketing.

Robert D. Buzzell
Frank M. Bass

PREFACE

The art and science of marketing are maturing rapidly. Advertising, for example, is now socially and emotionally oriented with a sharpness of focus not foreseen in the thirties and forties. The research techniques used in marketing today aim at uncovering a wide range of useful information. The selection of advertising media is subjected to an imposing number of sophisticated measurements of the depth, breadth, and quality of the audience. In the classrooms of colleges and universities and in books and periodicals, basic and advanced training in marketing is abundantly available. But the same sources that give so much information on most marketing areas give little on the use of sales promotion and merchandising.

There is no compendium on sales promotion and merchandising, and, in fact, source material on parts or the whole area is scattered and often incomplete. Hence this book. Written primarily as a textbook for students of business administration, it can also serve as a reference for practitioners. However, it is no more than a compilation of experience and a beginning of understanding.

This book attempts to answer the question of what the role of sales promotion and merchandising is in marketing. In the functioning of marketing, sales promotion and merchandising, like all other marketing activities, is part of the total effort, and sales promotion is part of selling, along with salesmanshhip and advertising. But sales promotion and merchandising differ from all other selling activities in that they aim at directly stimulating and motivating consumers to buy or attempt to make the channel of distribution put more effort into the marketing of a product or service.

As a compilation of experience, this book necessarily omits discussion of the imaginative aspects of sales promotion, because, however important, they are beyond its scope, although some of the examples offered are clearly very imaginative. Therefore, for one interested only in the imaginative aspects of sales promotion this book will not satisfy his needs, but for one interested in its functional aspects this book is for him.

This book is organized so that, with the exception of the two introductory chapters, each chapter is a unit. This allows students and practitioners to choose the topics of most interest to them. Specifically, Chapters 1 and 2 deal with what sales promotion and merchandising are and how they work.

The introductory chapters are followed by four chapters dealing with consumer sales promotion devices. Chapter 3 is concerned with introducing new or improved products, Chapter 4 with increasing the use of established products. In both chapters the emphasis is primarily on consumer motivation.

Chapter 5 deals with stimulating retailers. The sales promotion and merchandising devices that increase trade for retailers are important not only to them but also to manufacturers and wholesalers. The devices supplied to retailers are surely consumer-oriented, like those which attempt to stimulate business at the level of consumer commitment, that is, at the place of purchase.

In Chapter 6, we deal with increasing wholesalers' and retailers' marketing activities. These activities are important, because competition demands that the channel of distribution be stimulated, as well as consumers. The importance of this function of sales promotion has long been known by some manufacturers, but it has not been transmitted to the general trade or business public.

Chapter 7 deals with the legal aspects that affect sales promotion and merchandising. Government intervention in sales promotion has increased during the last few years, and the related legislation is complicated. The general principles are given in this chapter so that students and practitioners will have some guide as to what the law is, as well as a general survey of what can or cannot be done legally. The reader must be warned that this chapter is not a substitute for legal opinion or a guide to legal cases dealing with sales promotion; rather it is a brief descriptive analysis of legal concepts.

The authors are particularly indebted to Seton Hall University and the dean of the School of Business Administration, Robert J. Senkier, for his encouragement in helping make this work possible, as well as the many people in the trade who contributed something to it. We should especially like to thank Michael J. O'Connor, executive director of the Super Market Institute, Inc., who contributed importantly to this book and to the development of sales promotion as we know it; David G. Watrous, president of Luick & Watrous, Inc., for his counsel and encouragement; and the Reuben H. Donnelly Corporation, Marketing Division, Oak Brook, Illinois, for contributions to the sections on sampling and couponing.

John F. Luick
William Lee Ziegler

CONTENTS

SALES PROMOTION AND MODERN MERCHANDISING

PART 1/INTRODUCTION TO SALES PROMOTION AND MERCHANDISING

The nature of sales promotion and merchandising, and the place of these tools of promotion in marketing, are developed in the following introductory chapters. There, the definition of sales promotion and how it is organized within the marketing-orientated business firm is presented.

Sales promotion as a tool of marketing promotion gives rise to increase in product usage as well as expansion of markets for a product or introduction of a new product. The relationship of sales promotion devices to total marketing is the theme of this text.

Sales promotion and merchandising are not new endeavors in our marketing society. Some form of promotion which offered a premium or incentive to either the consumer or dealer has been a part of marketing since its inception. Today we have give-aways, contests, or premiums (which have become very sophisticated); prior to this, it was merchandise rather than money or premiums. What have changed in sales promotion and merchandising are the devices and not the concepts.

Sales promotion and merchandising have somewhat of a cyclical structure, that is, they come in and out of vogue. Trading stamps, which have been big in the sales promotion picture for the past few years, are probably on the wane, but the idea of the stamp plans will be used again. It will be the same for the contests which are now in vogue. They will fade out, either for lack of interest by the consumers or retailers or because of some kind of government restriction, and then rise again.

What keeps sales promotion going is the attitudes it stimulates in the consumers or dealers. Nothing is stronger to an individual than the feeling that he, the consumer, will receive something for nothing. The idea that something is free is the strongest selling point of sales promotion. The consumer's feeling of getting "something for nothing" may develop a commitment to the product or the retailer.

Sales promotion and merchandising have grown up in the last decade and have been accepted in the marketing scheme. As sales promotion devices become further integrated into the marketing mix, sales promotion will gain a place of greater acceptance.

CHAPTER 1/THE NATURE OF SALES PROMOTION

Common usage and modern merchandising practices identify sales promotion as a marketing force separate from advertising and personal selling. Among marketers who use sales promotion regularly, there is a general, if implicit, understanding of what the term means.

Taking the opinion of teachers as well as of businessmen into account the American Marketing Association defines the term as follows: [1]

> Sales Promotion. In a specific sense, those activities other than personal selling, advertising, and publicity, that stimulate consumer purchasing and dealer effectiveness, such as display, shows and exhibitions, demonstrations, and various nonrecurrent selling efforts not in the ordinary routine.

A similar definition is that of Albert Frey: [2]

> Sales promotion is concerned with the creation, application, and dissemination of materials and techniques that supplement advertising and personal selling. Sales promotion makes use of direct mail, catalogues, house organs, trade shows, sales contests, and other dealer aids. Its purpose is to increase the desire of salesmen, distributors, dealers to sell a certain brand and to make customers more eager to buy that brand. Personal selling and advertising can go only so far in these decisions: sales promotion provides an extra stimulus.

The goals of sales promotion are sales-force merchandising support, trade acceptance, and accelerated consumer purchasing. Sales promotion activates salesmen, encouraging them to make more solicitations and to build more product displays. New-customer contests, display contests, and incentives for exceeding sales quotas are elementary examples of sales promotion devices aimed at the sales force.

Sales promotion persuades a distributor or retailer to accept a product for sale and even to merchandise it aggressively. Sales promotion gains more shelf frontage for a new cereal and places a new clothes dryer in a better location on a retailer's selling floor.

Most important, sales promotion can trigger consumer

purchases. The premium offered with a product may encourage a consumer to try that product, thus creating a new and possibly loyal customer.

A more concise definition of sales promotion, which the authors of this text have devised, can now be given: A direct inducement which offers an extra value or incentive for the product to the sales force, distributors, or the ultimate consumer.

This, however, needs clarification. It is in the understanding of the words "an extra value or incentive" that we arrive at a delineation of the subject and still include all its elements. An extra value or incentive means that sales promotion adds to the worth of the purchase to the purchaser, regardless of who he is. This worth may be in the additional merchandise, price discount, or possible gain of such consumer sales promotion devices as premiums, price-off coupons, and contests.

Other sales promotion incentives are offered in the form of allowances of money or merchandise to the retailer or wholesaler. Point-of-purchase material, banners and posters, and window displays are added-value sales promotion incentives offered to retailers in order to influence potential customers.

The Pillsbury Bake-off is a sales promotion, not only because it is a contest for the entrants, but also because the winning recipes are offered as an added value to other customers as an incentive to purchase Pillsbury products. This is similar to consumer contests or sweepstakes in which consumers have to go to a retailer to get an entry blank. This sales promotion device is twofold: it is an added value to consumers in the contest and to retailers in the increased traffic in their store.

Sales promotion is also referred to as *direct inducement.* This means that it accomplishes certain specific marketing objectives by motivating and stimulating sales organizations, distributors and dealers, and consumers. Sales promotion through motivation and stimulation secures distribution for new products, product trial and repurchase, and reconversion of lost customers. Sales promotion sells leaf mulchers and snowplows to dealers before the autumn and winter demand. Sales promotion encourages purchasing for use in several places in the home—a cleaning compound for the kitchen and the laundry room. To the extent that sales promotion performs these functions it is one of the key components in the marketing plan.

There are two kinds of sales promotion: direct consumer stimulants and dealer and distributor stimulants.[3] Consumer sales promotion devices are: (1) Sampling, in order to introduce a new product or to expand the market. This gives consumers the opportunity to try the product. (2) Demonstrations or instructions on how the product is used. (3) Premium offers or temporary price reductions, which appeal to the bargain instinct. (4) Contests or sweepstakes for consumers, in order to stimulate interest in the product.

Dealer and distributor sales promotion devices are: (1) Helping dealers and distributors organize and manage their business by assisting them in planning and developing systems for their use. This includes store layout, accounting and inventory, and equipment and sales instruction. (2) Point-of-purchase promotions, which help dealers move more goods by displaying merchandise attractively. (3) Cooperative advertising programs, which either share the cost of advertising or supply the materials needed. (4) Dealer and distributor training for salesmen, which gives them a better knowledge of a product and how to show it. (5) Providing dealers and distributors with point-of-purchase premiums or money allowances that stimulate the buying of a manufacturer's products and customer goodwill for the dealer. (6) Money or merchandise allowances to stimulate dealers and distributors to take on a line of goods or to increase the amount of each purchase.

Selling the seller is an important part of marketing planning. This is particularly true in the appliance, automotive, and brewing industries, which invest heavily in sales promotion devices. It is estimated that the Joseph Schlitz Brewing Company spends $10 million or more a year on point-of-purchase materials, and Ford's Lincoln-Mercury division invests an estimated $6 million a year on training for its dealers' salesmen.[4]

Each form of sales promotion is aimed at moving products along the channel of distribution and enhancing their value or incentive to consumers as well as to the channel of distribution. Sales promotion brings the emphasis on distribution down to the local level. A consumer contest or sweepstakes for a European vacation in which the entry blank is obtained from local gasoline dealers is right down to grass roots. The contest or sweepstakes is aimed at the consumers but it also brings retailers into the sales promotion program.

Some historical background of sales promotion

There is no definitive history of sales promotion and very little reference material. However, sales promotion is found at almost every stage of history. William S. Beinecke, president of the Sperry and Hutchinson Company, reports: [5]

> As a matter of curiosity, we had some more scholarly friends dig into the history of this idea of something extra . . . that is, of something instead of nothing.
> Purchasers of ladies' cosmetic articles in ancient Rome, for example, were given free trinkets of extraordinary value, such as the gold-mounted tooth of a Hyrcanian wolf, or other magical charms guaranteed to help the woman win the heart of her secret love. Athenian idol manufacturers offered special free premiums—incense, lamps, and drinking cups—to the purchaser of an idol. Grecian garment makers gave special bracelets and ornaments to purchasers who spent a certain minimum amount. The indications are that premium inducements were practiced by the Oriental people thousands of years before the beginning of the Christian era.
> I remember when I visited Cairo 25 years ago with my Mother and Father. When visiting the bazaars, we were always offered a cup of coffee to drink with the proprietor before getting down to business.
> Here in America, many Colonial merchants found it to be in their long run interest to use the baker's dozen, to supply free needles with a purchase, or a peppermint stick for the customer's boy or girl.
> The general store in the rural community had the coffee

pot on the pot bellied stove, and the famous cracker barrel to be dipped into by local patrons.

In 1910 the *New York Sun* carried an interesting item. I quote: "News of grim, red-handed war comes to us from New Orleans where the retail grocers backed, we suppose, by the moral influence of the druggists, the marketmen, et cetera, are about to appeal to the legislature for a law prohibiting lagniappe and making the practice a misdemeanor.

"Lagniappe is a picturesque survival, the bestowal upon small purchasers of trivial donations, regulated by the size of the transaction, of gumdrops, candy and the like. They have tried to fight it by combination and mutual agreement, but they have failed. The institution is more than a hundred years old, and it dies hard, so after the modern fashion of running to the government on every trivial provocation, the grocers are about to ask the legislature to protect them against a custom of a century and a half's standing of inconsiderable importance in itself and so easily 'evened up' in practice as to make it negligible."

Beinecke was painting a background, not reciting history. However, because sales promotion became an identifiable marketing specialty only during the last few years, the lack of earlier history does not inhibit an understanding of it.

The practitioners of lagniappe may not have been sensitive to their local markets and promotion needs, but they would wonder at the variety and complexity of modern sales promotion. Although there is a little evidence of maturation in the practice during the years between 1920 and 1940, it was not until after World War II that sales promotion became a carefully planned and executed marketing procedure.

There are a number of influences that brought about the development of modern sales promotion. The first was economic growth. If there is a single fundamental principle governing sales promotion, it is that promotions increase in number and strength as goods become more abundant and, conversely, that they decrease in time of scarcity.

At the end of World War II, the nation's production had to be converted to the manufacture of consumer goods. This took several years, and during this time there was little sales promotion, because there was little need for it. Goods were in short supply. One waited four to six months for a new automobile and paid full list price. Appliances were scarce, and so were certain foods. Slowly a war-oriented product capability was altered, and in a few short years scarcity was replaced by surplus. Then manufacturers offered premiums to make their product attractive to consumers. Grocers had weekend specials, consumer contests, and eventually trading stamps. Sales promotion had arrived as a major marketing force.

A second influence in the development of sales promotion was the changing political climate and its legal expressions. The antitrust acts were passed to protect competition and restrict discrimination against small businessmen in favor of larger competitors. The antitrust acts—the Sherman act, the Clayton act, and the Robinson-Patman act—forced a change of emphasis from pricing to sales promotion on sellers. Pricing discrimination was made illegal by the antitrust acts, and this gave rise to abuses of restraints of trade through sales promotion. These abuses were similar to those practiced in pricing in that they discriminated in money and merchandising allowances for sales promotion, and so the antitrust acts were amended to cope with these new problems. By accident the legal control of the antitrust acts formed the restrictive controls of sales promotion.

A third and perhaps the strongest influence on sales promotion was a greater sophistication in marketing. The development of competition among similar products, which resulted in branding, changed the whole nature of sales promotion. Branding and changes in retailing brought about consumer self-selection, which affected packaging through the need for distinctiveness. Because of competition and packaging another means was necessary to make consumers purchase a particular brand. Something had to be added to the product that was not part of it. This need was met by sales promotion, which gave the product an added value—added value necessary to make the consumer purchase brand A instead of brand B. This, in turn, gave distributors and retailers an incentive to purchase for resale.

The last influence on sales promotion was the ability to select and apply specific uses for sales promotion devices. Accumulated experience, the history of success and failure, could be applied in future planning. The ability to audit sales promotion results in retail sales figures through specialized data processing and research services—A. C. Nielsen Co., Market Research Corporation of America, and others—and through other auditing programs has added a healthy objectivity to analysis, which previously had been quite subjective. Computers are used to evaluate sales promotion, and they will undoubtedly add further sophistication to marketing.

The relationship of sales promotion to other marketing activities

After World War II the marketing structure of the more advanced American corporations matured. Most corporations were originally orientated to production; but the emphasis changed, and they stressed first sales and then marketing. However, this change of emphasis did not affect corporate structure uniformly. Some organizations adopted the brand-manager system, in which an individual is assigned the task of managing the marketing of a product or a group of products. Others decentralized and placed responsibility with sales regions or divisions. And others varied or combined these plans. Because of variety in structure and differences in responsibility it is difficult, if not impossible, to place sales promotion in a typical corporate organization.

But is it necessary to do so? Not according to Albert Frey, who says that the authority relationship in corporations is not so important as the communications relationship.[6] Who talks with whom is more important than who reports to whom, and the communications relationship is most important to sales promotion function.

With whom, then, should sales promotion talk in a manufacturing corporation? Communication for sales promotion may be divided into primary and secondary channels.

Primary channels of communication for sales promotion The primary channels of communication for sales promotion connect the marketing functions of a manufacturer, usually under the immediate supervision of a marketing director. There are three primary channels.

The first and most important is between sales promotion and brand management. These two departments activate the sales promotion plan by establishing a set of objectives [7] that should be compatible with those of marketing. If marketing objectives aim at trading up customers to a larger size of a product, then sales promotion should not aim at repeat purchase of a smaller size.

Sales promotion objectives should, if possible, be expressed in terms of quantity. An objective of trading up customers to larger sizes of a product is not so precisely stated as one that calls for increasing unit sales on the two larger sizes of a product from 26 to 32 percent of total unit sales. Still more precise is a statement of the proposed sales increase on each size.

Another important matter concerning objectives is the sales promotion budget, which is determined by the brand management and the sales promotion departments. This matter also includes the scheduling of sales promotions and the use of advertising or other support for the campaign.

The second primary channel of communication is between sales promotion and advertising, which are both mass means of stimulating and motivating consumers to buy a product. Sales promotion and advertising should harmonize to be effective,[8] and sales promotion should be timed and oriented so as to complement advertising. Many food and beverage companies use a health-and-energy approach in advertising. This naturally leads to radio and television sponsorship of sporting events and to the use of premiums, contests, and point-of-purchase merchandising with a sports theme. The Gillette Razor Company customarily gives a sports premium, usually a record book, with its sponsorship of the radio and television broadcast of the World Series.

Communication between advertising and sales promotion is also important because advertising may act as the carrier of a sales promotion. Coupons often appear in the body of an advertisement, and contests and sweepstakes are sometimes the main or only subject matter of an advertisement. The entire advertisement, in such cases, aims at soliciting entries in the contest or sweepstakes by pointing out the value, attractiveness, or number of prizes offered. There is little or no message dealing with the product itself.

The third primary channel of communication is between sales promotion and sales. Sales letters, brochures, and fact sheets must be sent to the sales force so that the nature and details of the sales promotion device are clearly understood by the salesmen and their customers. To implement sales promotion in the field, a description of each sales promotion device, plus an indication of terms, discounts, effective dates, and other elementary data, must be announced.

The sales force is the contact between the manufacturer and the channel of distribution, and the distributor may also communicate the promotion still further: to the retailer, for example. The sales force must not only be informed of the promotion but must also be able to support and justify it.

The key to the success of any sales promotion device that uses distributors and retailers is the support that it receives from them. Without it the sales promotion cannot reach its potential.[9] An example is a combination offer in which consumers receive a sample of mouthwash with the purchase of a tube of a specific brand of toothpaste. This sales promotion device will be successful only if retailers give it good display and help push the toothpaste.

Secondary channels of communication for sales promotion

There are also secondary channels of communication for developing the cooperation of a company in devising sales promotion plans. If the primary channels concern the merchandising strategy and tactics of sales promotion, then the secondary ones concern its legality and feasibility.

Legal clearance should be obtained for every sales promotion device planned. The extent of the laws affecting sales promotion is wide and varied, and there is little agreement on many interpretations. The loss and harassment resulting from questionable sales promotion make it necessary to have information and opinions from one's legal advisors before any plans are implemented. Today the Federal Trade Commission is examining the legality of bingo consumer contests, and before starting such a contest as a sales promotion device, a company should be familiar with the legal implications of the commission's findings.

Other Federal as well as state agencies have jurisdiction over what can be done in sales promotion. The post office has jurisdiction over what can be mailed, and through its Mailability Division, is very cooperative in giving opinions regarding the acceptability of sales promotion devices, particularly contests and sweepstakes.

Less obvious, but equally important, local restrictions on sales promotion should be considered. A state may forbid sweepstakes. In fact, as of this writing, two states, Nebraska and Wisconsin, do so. Cities and counties may also have laws that inhibit or forbid certain kinds of sales promotion devices or methods of distribution. Usually an internal legal department can rule on their legality. However, appropriate external sources, such as specialized sales promotion consultants, are often more alert to potential danger and can offer good advice.

The market research department, often internal, should be consulted on sales promotion plans that need testing and evaluation. It may not be necessary to call for research on every sales promotion proposal; but frequently special studies are in order, and it is not unusual for an alert market research department to recognize an opportunity to combine several projects for simultaneous processing. Such potential savings in time and money are often available through a central market research facility and are well worth seeking out.

Another secondary channel of communication for sales promotion is with production. In all manufacturing companies where sales promotion affects production, this communication is essential. If a promotion needs a certain size of a product or another product as a premium, production will be involved. If the promotion will affect only sales, production should still be informed so that they can adjust their scheduling.

Engineering is another important checkpoint for sales promotion personnel. Engineering is concerned with changes in the normal flow of production. Often a proposed sales promotion device requires changes in package weight or fill and in package size, which, in turn, require changes in shipping and perhaps in conveyor or chute clearance and aspects of machinery performance. Free samples usually require changes in shipping and handling methods because of changes in the size of packaging.

The packaging experts should also be briefed on sales promotion. Many promotion devices require extensive packaging adjustments. Side-by-side deals, in which two packages are banded together, are often given as a premium. Plastic blisters are used when product or premium visibility is desired. A boot is another kind of sales promotion package. Shown above is an illustration of a free sample of syrup attached to a box of pancake mix by means of a boot. In this instance, the heavy weight of the sample, its unusual cruet shape, and the use of glass as a container were a difficult challenge to packaging. A strong and functional boot was developed—one that also yielded the opportunity for good graphic presentation of the product itself.

In many cases, a sales promotion package also becomes a channel of communication between a company and consumers. In this form of sales promotion, selling copy is placed on the package itself. "Free Inside" or "See Package Back for Details" are common examples. If this form of communication is used, then the package has to be designed to accommodate it.

The traffic department should be consulted on any problems of shipping and mailing, because there may be changes in freight rates or mailing procedures. In 1962 and 1963, such a problem occurred with a sales promotion device very much in vogue. At that time there was a fad of inserting real coins in packages instead of marking "Cents Off." Although the weight of the coins caused no problem, freight rates for shipping money were quite different from those for more ordinary merchandise and affected the cost of the sales promotion.

In any company there may also be other departments that should be informed of sales promotion plans, and these other departments would then be considered the secondary channels of communication for sales promotion.

Obstacles to successful sales promotion

Sales promotion offers many opportunities to manufacturers, but there are obstacles to its most effective use. The first is slow operation and decision making. The fact that many departments in a corporation must be consulted on a sales promotion device retards its implementation. Changes suggested by the legal department may need to be relayed to an advertising-agency copywriter. He, in turn, may rewrite an advertisement and consult artists and others on the advertising-agency staff before submitting the changes to the client. All this may take several weeks, but it is only one of many possible delays.

Another obstacle is the conservatism of older companies. Many young companies have to take risks that older ones cannot. This is especially true in sales promotion, where the risks are not only in money but also in reputation. Although growth is always desirable, an established organization must first protect its position. This discourages adventure, which is the key to the development of new kinds of sales promotion.

In spite of these problems sales promotion serves many needs of manufacturers of consumer goods. These needs can best be expressed in terms of the objectives of sales promotion: [10]

1. To introduce a new product
2. To increase the inventories of distributors and dealers
3. To increase a product's use by present customers
4. To attract new customers
5. To counter a competitor's sales promotion device or other marketing activities
6. To reduce the extent of a seasonal decline
7. To make it easier for salesmen to secure more shelf space and place point-of-purchase displays in retail stores

For new products, the sales promotion objectives are two-fold: to reach consumers—to motivate and stimulate them to purchase a product—and to induce distributors and dealers to carry it. Either of these objectives can be accomplished by many devices, but the most common are samples and premiums for consumers and money or merchandise allowances for distributors and dealers.

An important objective of sales promotion is to increase the amount of a product that distributors and dealers carry in their inventories. This gives manufacturers better coverage of the market as well as economy in supplying buyers. Distributors and especially retailers are reluctant to carry large quantities of a product unless they feel that they can move it in a short time. Such dealer stimulants as money or merchandise deals, dealer loaders, and displays help increase the inventory that retailers and distributors are willing and able to absorb.

Another objective of sales promotion is to increase the use of a product by present customers. This is done by introducing new applications for it. Demonstrations and contests are the most common means. Pillsbury's Bake-off is a good example. As the contest develops new recipes, they are distributed to consumers who, hopefully, will use Pillsbury products in these new ways.

All marketing activities are aimed at attracting the widest possible market for a product. By drawing consumers to a product with premiums, samples, and contests and sweepstakes, sales promotion supplies the incentive to consumers to try products that they have not used before and also to try the products that are given as the added value.

Risk enters into a consumer's decision to buy a product not tried before: [11]

> Consumer behavior involves risk in the sense that any action of a consumer will produce consequences which he cannot anticipate with anything approximating certainty, and some of which at least are likely to be unpleasant. At the very least, any one purchase competes for the consumer's financial resources with a vast array of alternate uses of that money.

The added value of premiums, samples, and coupons gives consumers something more for their money, a bargain. This reduces the risk, because they feel they are getting more than they are entitled to. In demonstrations the risk is reduced by showing consumers how a product will work for them.

Sales promotion is also used to counter the introduction of competitive products, product improvements, and competitive sales promotions. If we examine the me-tooism of the gasoline companies' recent consumer games, we see how this was used to oppose competitive promotions.[12] Tidewater Oil started it all with its Win-a-Check game, followed by Shell Oil, and at its height at least 17 companies offered games simply to compete with Tidewater and Shell. They had to, to protect their business.

But sales promotion is also used to counter other marketing activities. Devices, such as premiums, price-off coupons, and contests and sweepstakes, counter advertising and price reductions. Combination offers help defend against the introduction of new competitive brands. In dealer sales promotions, competition is almost the byword, because it is used so often.

Products of a seasonal nature present another problem to manufacturers. Sales promotion is used to lengthen the season of use for a product and give it new uses or make it fashionable in other seasons. Using a sales promotion device that emphasizes the larger size of a product helps lengthen its season of use. A hot breakfast cereal realizes additional tonnage from a sales promotion on a large package in March or early April. The Campbell Soup Company has increased the length of its season by promoting its prepared soups in other than cold weather by suggesting new or other uses for them.

Finally, sales promotion is used to give salesmen more leverage in obtaining shelf and floor space for point-of-purchase displays. Through the use of dealer loaders and dealer stimulants of any kind salesmen have the opportunity, not only to sell retailers, but also to insist on better display and help in merchandising at this level.[13]

These are the objectives of sales promotion in marketing. The use of sales promotion devices should be suitable to a company's marketing policy and planning. What is important is that sales promotion helps in almost all marketing situations. Its basic strength is at the consumer level, that is, moving goods to consumers, but because many sales promotion devices depend on retail cooperation, retailers cannot be ignored.

The potentialities of sales promotion have been examined, but the limitations should also be stated. Indeed, most failures in sales promotion can be traced to the application of a good sales promotion device to an objective that could only be reached by different marketing methods:

1. Sales promotion cannot build a consumer franchise for a product. This is the function of advertising or, more often, of the total marketing effort. Because it is temporary and is oriented to a particular retail buying action, sales

promotion alone is not sufficient to execute long-range strategy.

2. Sales promotion cannot compensate for any product deficiencies. Sales promotion may delay the decline of a faltering product, but, in these cases, the delay is not a permanent solution. Too often sales promotion is given the almost impossible task of rescuing a product that has not responded to advertising or has not been improved in the laboratory.

3. Sales promotion alone cannot overcome major marketing errors. A poorly packaged, poorly sized product, an off-target product marketing strategy—these and other mistakes cannot be corrected solely by sales promotion.

In sales promotion there is a saturation level, and it is often lower than merchandisers know. Used consistently, or even intermittently, too many sales promotions weaken any marketing effort. A proper balance is needed between sales promotion and total marketing, and this can only come from marketing management.

Notes

1. *Marketing Definitions: A Glossary of Marketing Terms,* American Marketing Association, Chicago, 1960, p. 20.

2. Albert W. Frey, "Promotion," a Special Supplement to *Business Horizons,* Indiana University, Bloomington, Ind., February, 1961.

3. William J. Schultz, *American Marketing,* Wadsworth Publishing Company, Inc., San Francisco, 1961, p. 435.

4. " 'Selling the Sellers' Is Big-time Action," *Advertising Age,* Dec. 12, 1966, p. 56.

5. William S. Beinecke, Tobe lecture series, Harvard University, Feb. 15, 1962.

6. Albert W. Frey, Speech before the Association of National Advertisers, New York, March, 1965.

7. Lewis K. Johnson, *Sales and Marketing Management,* Allyn and Bacon, Inc., Boston, 1957, pp. 540–541. This author divides

the functions of sales promotion into four major groupings, which he subdivides into 42 parts.

8. John B. Mathews, Jr., et al., *Marketing: An Introductory Analysis*, McGraw-Hill Book Company, New York, 1964, p. 410.

9. Ralph S. Alexander and Thomas L. Berg, *Dynamic Management in Marketing*, Richard D. Irwin, Inc., Homewood, Ill., 1965, p. 385.

10. Mathews et al., *op. cit.*, p. 385.

11. Raymond A. Bauer, "Consumer Behavior as Risk Taking," in Robert S. Hancock (ed.), *Proceedings of the 43rd National Conference of the American Marketing Association*, Chicago, June 15–17, 1960, p. 392.

12. "Oil Marketers Drop Bingo Promotions as Burgeoning Games Lose Initial Zip," *Advertising Age,* Dec. 12, 1966, p. 1.

13. "Dealer Loaders, Prizes, Gifts, Spur Selling," *Advertising Age,* Dec. 12, 1966, p. 39.

CHAPTER 2 / SALES PROMOTION POLICY AND ORGANIZATION

Modern marketing reaches a high point with the development of appropriate advertising, sales, and sales promotion programs, and a well-directed marketing program correlates all a company's selling efforts. Specifically the primary purpose of sales promotion is to implement the plans of a manufacturer's sales personnel, advertising, and distributors and dealers in the channel of distribution in order to obtain maximum selling and to reach specific consumers with sales promotion.[1]

Immediately after World War II manufacturers of consumer goods considered it sufficient to produce a desirable product, advertise it to consumers, and have salesmen call on distributors and dealers. They soon learned, however, that using only advertising and selling left gaps in marketing management programs.

Relying wholly on advertising as a means of stimulating consumer demand proved inadequate for most manufacturers. Although advertising attracts consumers, motivates desire, breaks down resistance, and in some cases presells consumers, in general, advertising is too broad an approach. It is not and cannot be used alone but must be part of a larger marketing plan.

The nature of the American marketing system, in which distributors and retailers handle the products of many manufacturers, is such that manufacturers lose the direct sales approach. Their approach is not to consumers, the users of the products, but to distributors and retailers who sell to retailers and consumers. In this situation, manufacturers must rely on the selling efforts of retailers to move goods.

And they also rely on retailers to advertise their products. But retailers handle the products of many manufacturers and cannot be expected to advertise those of only one. In fact, retailers advertise in order to increase traffic into their stores and not necessarily to stimulate demand for a specific product.[2]

Manufacturers must therefore supplement retail advertising and selling methods with efforts that stimulate and motivate consumers. They must either bypass retailers completely and reach consumers directly or use retailers to do so for them. In either case manufacturers must supplement their marketing programs with strong sales promotion devices that will make consumers buy.[3]

Sales promotion planning

Regardless of the level or function of a business operation, planning is its most important aspect. The aspects of business organizational planning are (1) the goal, (2) the allocation of resources, (3) the method of evaluation, and (4) the relationship of business organization to other activities.

The factors of planning for a business organization must also hold for any part of the business function. Therefore, sales promotion must also have planning. Sales promotion needs a goal, a means of allocation of resources, must be able to be evaluated, and must work in harmony with the other factors or facets of the business organization.

The goal of sales promotion Although the general purpose of sales promotion, like all other marketing activities, is to increase sales, its specific purpose depends on how it is used. Whom a sales promotion is directed to and how it is being transmitted determine its goal.

There are three forms of sales promotion: two aimed at consumers and another at the channel of distribution. But the two aimed at consumers do not have the same specific goal. One of them is communicated directly to the consumer, and its purpose is to increase the sale of the product being promoted.

Another form of sales promotion is aimed at consumers through the retailers with whom they deal, and its goal is to make consumers buy a product at a specific retailer's place of business. Although this form of promotion increases the sale of the product, as in the first method, it also helps a specific retailer, and this is a different goal. This form of sales promotion has the goal of increasing the sales of the product at specific retail locations.

A third form of sales promotion induces wholesalers and retailers to handle a line of goods and then to promote it more actively. This form of promotion increases sales, but its specific goal is to motivate and stimulate the channel of distribution.

Another analysis of goals could be made of how sales promotion helps a product become established or strengthened in the marketplace. Certain forms of sales promotion, like samples, premiums, and contests and sweepstakes, are used to introduce a product to consumers or to a new marketing area. The goal of such sales promotion devices is to make consumers try a product and continue to use it.

Other forms of sales promotion are used to support a product in competitive situations. Cents-off coupons and price-off promotions are examples. Such devices are bargains, and they make consumers repurchase a product even in the face of strong competitive marketing. Bargains keep a product moving in the marketplace and defend it against competition.

Allocation of resources   The allocation of resources is another aspect to planning sales promotion programs. This includes (1) the procedure for recording and administering expenditures and (2) the more difficult decision regarding the amount of money to be spent on sales promotion generally and, specifically, on particular sales promotion devices.

Budgets are most often recorded on the basis of account numbers assigned to various expenditures that are tabulated in the accounting or budget control department. If account number 25 is assigned to radio advertising, each brand manager or advertising manager charges his expenditure for radio advertising to this number. For each product and for all products, radio expenditures can be located and identified in account number 25. For the purpose of administering the budgets, a monthly form may be issued by the accounting or budget control department to help control expenditures.

A simplified and abbreviated example of such a report follows:

Form 66

April 5, 1968

PRODUCT NAME
SALES PROMOTION BUDGET
FOR YEAR ENDING JULY 31, 1968

EXPENDITURES

ACCOUNT NUMBER	ACTIVITY	BUDGET	9 MONTHS TO DATE	COMMITTED	AMOUNT OVER (UNDER) BUDGET
26	Samples	$ 80,000	$ 40,000	$ 30,000	$ 10,000 –
27	P.O.P. material	120,000	80,000	20,000	20,000 –
28	Premiums	20,000	17,000	6,000	3,000 +
29	Consumer contests				
30	Co-op allowances	70,000	30,000	40,000	0
31	Coupon redemption	280,000	255,000	12,000	13,000 –

Many other reports and forms may be used as aids in sales promotion administration. Quarterly, semiannual, and annual reports of expenditures are among those commonly used. Reports and estimates of coupon and premium redemptions are also helpful in planning budgets. However, the basic form, as illustrated above, or another one listing the same information is the heart of administering and budgeting a sales promotion plan.

More important to planning is the determination of the share of the total marketing budget for sales promotion. Sales promotion is usually considered a part of the total promotion program, including advertising and publicity, and therefore sales promotion must compete with advertising and publicity for its share of the available funds. For most products, this is a continually debated question—how much for each part of the promotion campaign.

Even when there is an abundance of marketing history for study and guidance, experimentation with various amounts of sales promotion expenditure should continue. Frequency of sales promotion, kind of device, and allocation of funds are factors that need continual testing; for the marketplace changes, and sales promotion responds quickly to changes in retail and wholesale patterns.

The frequency of sales promotion is directly affected by the amount of money available. The cost of every sales promotion device must be proportionate to the return expected and the money available. Today in marketing there is a heavy emphasis on competitive sales promotion in which companies go into it, not as an allocation of resources, but as a competitive measure. The use of defensive competitive measures leads to a frequency of sales promotion that is not justified by an analysis of the allocation of resources.

Even when there is long-range information on the value of sales promotion, companies still need an analysis of the devices that work best for their products. Typically experts in sales promotion hold that sampling is a good device for the introduction of new products. But is this true for all products in all areas in dissimilar marketing situations? Any good practitioner of marketing says that every case is different and generalizations about the use of sales promotion devices are of little value. Therefore companies must analyze sales promotion devices and fit them to the goal and the strategy of their program for the best results in the allocation of resources.

To illustrate the difficulty of allocating a percentage of promotion funds in a marketing budget, let us first agree that generalities are of little value. There is no sure formula for successful products. Many important brands of soap, mustard, pickles, hedge clippers, lawn mowers, hosiery, and lingerie are not heavily promoted but are highly successful. The shelves of supermarkets, hardware stores, and department stores are full of brands that sell well with sales promotion only.[4] However, the same shelves are heavy with brands whose great success can be traced to persuasive advertising.

A rule may not be practical for the allocation of sales promotion funds, but it may be said that sales promotion increases in importance as the urgency of the marketing of a product requires. A new product may be sampled at a cost of $3 million in its first year, but later this sales promotion may more than reverse itself when the immediate need for sampling has been satisfied. A faltering product may need heavy investment in sales promotion. A product under unusual attack from competition may require strong sales promotion. A new product, a faltering product, and a highly competitive product are in a temporary situation, and the needs of the product in these situations are satisfied by the help that temporary sales promotion devices can give. Funds for these temporary situations are usually only a small part of the total marketing budget, but an important part nevertheless.

Evaluation of sales promotion   The importance of the accurate evaluation of sales promotion cannot be overemphasized. It is no longer sufficient to judge sales promotion devices as good or bad, success or failure. Parts of a sales promotion program may be effective, and others not; but under certain marketing conditions, a relatively small degree of success may be acceptable in the total marketing program.

A weak mail-in offer is an acceptable effort in an otherwise strong product introduction. Thus degrees of success must be considered, as well as the relationship of the sales promotion to other forces of communication. As informative as sales promotion evaluation is, it is still used far too seldom, and, when used, it often produces misleading generalities instead of meaningful specifics about the effect of the device. To get the most helpful information, evaluation should be provided for in the original plan. It should not be an afterthought. The method, the timing, and the reports involved in evaluating sales promotion should be an integral part of the total marketing plan.

In evaluating sales promotion, the first step is to restate the specific sales promotion goals, because the success of the promotion will be measured against their attainment.[5] Elementary or not, the measurement of sales promotion in the light of its own objectives is often overlooked. Even so uncomplicated a device as a booth at a trade show or convention should be evaluated by its ability to meet certain stated objectives. Should the booth build general goodwill or help salesmen write orders? Should it communicate an idea of progress or aggressiveness on the part of its sponsor? Should it tell a story of success in new products or try to spotlight some of a manufacturer's less well-known ones? Should it demonstrate a new merchandising technique for the conventioneers? Booths may be judged on their physical attractiveness, their ability to stop traffic, and other superficial bases. A truly useful judgment, however, is based on the ability of the booth to do what it was supposed to. This is true for the evaluation of any form of sales promotion.

To evaluate a sales promotion device, a complete description of the program is needed. This is a restatement of a part of the marketing plan, and it should be found there. The basic elements of a good sales promotion plan should contain:

1. Starting and closing dates of the sales promotion device

2. Confines or restrictions on the shipping dates

3. Anticipated date for its appearance on the shelves or floors of dealers or delivery to consumers

4. Regional variations in dates or terms of the sales promotion, if any

5. Details on dates and kinds of advertising, direct-mail, or point-of-purchase material that will support the promotion

6. Nature and extent of the offer or deal

7. Instructions to the sales force on how to handle the device

8. Anticipated costs of each element of the promotion

9. Recapitulation of competitive promotion activity and changes in competitive advertising and merchandising

The next step in the evaluation of sales promotion, also a part of the marketing plan, is to decide what measurements will be applied to the device and how and when they will be used. There are, in practice, many measurements available.

Sales volume, compared with that of the competition—its brand share—can be measured in total or by size of package. Shipments from plants and factories can be counted. Field surveys can measure the effects of a sales promotion on overall distribution or, when needed, on distribution by kind, size, and location of outlet. A promotion's effect on retail and wholesale pricing can be learned from audits and special sales-force reports. Successful sales promotions usually cause an out-of-stock condition. Field reports of all kinds should require information on this not uncommon problem. Field sales personnel might also report on price, display and advertising, and other in-store support. Retail attitudes toward specific sales promotions can also be discovered, although it should be kept in mind that a retailer's negative attitude does not *ipso facto* mean that he will reject a sales promotion device. Retailers almost invariably object to off-label sales promotions, but they often support them aggressively.

A count of the movement of merchandise and an assessment of retailer cooperation can be obtained by standard retail audits, special retail audits, sales-force reports, and field trips by home-office personnel. But to measure the effectiveness of sales promotions with consumers is more difficult in most cases. Responses to mail-in refund offers and free-in-the-mail premium requests can be counted. Many measurements can lead to conclusions about the general value of a sales promotion. However, more sophisticated and generally helpful information is not easily obtained.

The information needed to evaluate a consumer sales promotion device may include the number of product users developed by a sample or price-off coupon, the number of the competition's customers captured by a price promotion or premium offer, and the effect on new products of sales promotions of the entire brand.

Manufacturers are also interested in which sales promotion devices get better results. Are new buyers attracted by frequent short promotions or fewer long ones? Are certain sales promotion devices more successful with consumers of certain income levels, educational backgrounds, and the like? Can brands with a stronger consumer franchise use weaker sales promotion devices successfully? Do customers won by a specific sales promotion device remain regular users, or do they return to their old brand after the sales promotion is over?

Most often this information can only be discovered by consumer-research studies especially created to obtain specific data. Consumer sales promotion research is costly and is often justified only for those devices that are to have a major influence on a brand or are so costly that analysis is clearly desirable. Thus, the expense involved limits the use of this method of evaluation.

The final step is the actual evaluation process. Has the sales promotion device achieved its specific and prestated goal? Let us examine a hypothetical but not unusual sales promotion. A manufacturer has a window cleaner that retails for 44 cents in grocery stores. In order to gain new customers, he plans and executes a 5-cents-off-label sales promotion to bring the price of his product down to an attractive 39 cents. His objective is a 15 percent increase in volume, two-thirds of which would be from new customers (a level of performance lower than a 15 percent increase would not pay). On the basis of experience he is confident that new customers will continue to buy his brand of window cleaner.

The manufacturer audits the market for two months before the sales promotion starts, counting retail sales and brand share. He then audits it during the sales promotion and finds that his product actually has an 18 percent increase in sales. However, postsales promotion audits show that it has only a small fraction of this volume two months later.

Fortunately, the manufacturer institutes research to trace the success with new customers. The research discloses that the price-off device stimulated his present customers to buy several packages of his product because of the discount but that the sales promotion was not strong enough or of the proper kind to make others who were satisfied with competitive products try his.

This sales promotion device with superficially good results failed in its attempt to obtain new customers. The goal was not to increase sales for a short time but to attract new customers.

Cost should also be evaluated in the postanalysis of sales promotion devices. Not only the overall cost, but also the cost per new customer, cost per larger size sold, cost per display obtained, cost versus other sales promotions or similar previous ones, and the like. It is in these two areas that sales promotion evaluation must be conducted—the ability of sales promotion to achieve its goals at a cost that produces a reasonable profit through immediate or repeat sales.

Relationship of sales promotion to other marketing functions

Personal selling is usually the responsibility of the sales manager. The sales manager is interested in the salesmen's relationship with customers; the advertising manager, on the other hand, in the mass selling effort. The sales manager puts his faith in personal contact; the advertising manager believes in the nonpersonal contact of mass promotion. The advertising manager is a specialist who directs advertising through established mass media, such as newspapers, magazines, radio, television, billboards, and the like.

The sales promotion manager fills the gaps left by the sales and advertising departments while enhancing the effectiveness of personal selling and advertising. Much of what the sales promotion department does overlaps what selling and advertising do, but this overlap is necessary to get a good marketing and promotional blend.[6]

Salesmanship, advertising, and sales promotion usually attempt to reach the same people. Because customers for a product cannot be classified precisely or reached by any one means of promotion, there has to be overlap.

There is also overlap because of the need to reach customers more than once. The duplication of message by three different departments strengthens willingness to purchase and is not wasteful.

Overlapping of salesmanship, advertising, and sales promotion is also necessary when one of the methods of stimulating customers lacks strength or cannot reach the audience desired. Personal selling may not affect consumers but may affect retailers who sell a product. Here salesmen show retailers how important the promotion is in helping them sell the product.

The interaction of salesmanship, advertising, and sales promotion, called the marketing or promotional blend, moves a product to consumers through more than one channel or vehicle of promotional communication.

Integration of sales promotion with the channel of distribution

The main purpose of sales promotion is to increase the sale of a product or the traffic in a retail store. That is, sales promotion attempts to stimulate consumers directly to purchase a product or to go to a certain retailer, not to purchase a particular product, but to take advantage of a premium, contest, or temporary price discount. Sales promotion is also used to stimulate dealers to do a better job in merchandising products through dealer contests, dealer loaders, and price deals and allowances. Each of these devices affects, not only consumers, but also wholesalers and retailers in the channel of distribution.

The effects of sales promotion devices on consumers are important to sales promotion usage and the amount of support obtained from the channel of distribution. Remember that what is good for the manufacturer in a sales promotion program must also be good for dealers and distributors, who, otherwise, may not be willing to cooperate.

There are two kinds of consumer sales promotion device: those which reach consumers at home and those which reach them in retail stores. Devices that go into the home attempt to presell consumers on the product or brand. These devices attempt to give them a reason for purchase before going to a retailer. There are four kinds: samples, coupons, contests, and demonstrations.[7]

In-store sales promotion devices attempt to reach consumers at the place of purchase; they include short-run price reductions (price-off), premium offers, demonstrations, and point-of-purchase displays. These devices help influence purchasing and also build up traffic for retailers.

The role of retailers in handling in-store sales promotion devices should be examined. Naturally they want consumer traffic and the increase in sales that it generates. But when a device also increases his costs, a retailer is reluctant to handle it.

Some sales promotions benefit retailers greatly, although they carry them at a heavy expense. Included in this category are trading stamps, used widely by food retailers and gasoline stations, and consumer contests and sweepstakes. Both these devices are costly to retailers, who pay for trading stamps at an average cost of 2 to 3 percent of sales and, for contests and sweepstakes, at an average cost of about 2 cents per entry blank. Many retailers are forced into devices of this kind simply for competitive reasons, because a retailer across the street institutes them.

Sales promotions that attempt to stimulate dealers to handle and push the products of a manufacturer include dealer contests, dealer loaders, merchandise and promotion allowances, dealer sales training, and point-of-purchase displays.

Each of these devices requires support from retailers, in time or space, both important considerations to the retailer. Dealers naturally view these devices from the standpoint of how they affect retailers and their business, as well as themselves. Many sales promotion devices bring open disapproval from retailers, because they cannot be justified by increased sales or retailers cannot be concerned with the problems that these devices create.

Many retailers are openly against sales contests for their sales personnel. Retailers do not want salesmen to sell a line of branded goods instead of showing the merchandise that they have to offer. Retailers are more interested in matching customers with the goods that they want. This is the reason for the wide selection of merchandise that retailers carry. They are not interested in selling customers a particular item but in selling them something. Sales-force contests attempt to push a line of goods rather than sell the goods of a retailer. Therefore many retailers feel that sales personnel contests do them a disservice.

Other dealer promotion devices create similar problems that affect retailers adversely, in fact or in their mind. Dealer loaders and displays are often large and clumsy and cannot be handled easily; training sessions must be held at odd hours, and sometimes this causes employee problems, or, worse, salesmen have to be taken from the selling floor; merchandise deals often tax retailers' storage facilities, creating an overloaded and unbalanced stock.

All in all, there are problems as well as benefits with each of the sales promotion devices aimed at retailers, and retailers must weigh the pros and cons. The attitude of retailers is also determined by the size and type of their business and the buying habits of the consumers who frequent their store.

Sales promotion devices affect wholesalers much differently. Wholesalers are in the middle of the channel of distribution, but sales promotion devices are more clearly aimed at the end of the line. Although anything that helps the movement of the total amount of goods has a beneficial effect on the whole channel, it is sometimes difficult for wholesalers to see how end-of-the-line sales promotion devices indirectly benefit them.

There are three major practical sales promotion devices used to stimulate wholesalers: contests, either for wholesalers themselves or their sales personnel; merchandise deals; and money allowances—the second and third aimed directly at wholesalers. All three create problems similar to those of retailers. These devices consume time and space, and there are administrative problems involved in handling them. Although contests, merchandise allowances, and money allowances are used and are profitable, particularly to manufacturers, distributors feel sometimes that the devices are not worthwhile.

The difficult situation with sales promotion devices and wholesalers is that in many cases wholesalers are also the functioning agent or representative of a manufacturer in the handling and operation of the device, and they are required to interest retailers in its use. This is a burden on wholesalers and directly affects their sales and service personnel. The practice, however, is common.

The usual sales promotion devices handled by wholesalers are point-of-purchase material, premiums, coupons, and merchandise and money allowances. With the exception of merchandise deals and money allowances, which can be considered a sales inducement to retailers, all the devices are a sales service to manufacturers, and wholesalers attempt to get retailer support for them. Most of these devices are not strong enough to stimulate retailers to purchase the goods in order to take advantage of the sales promotion.

The reluctance of wholesalers and retailers to take on promotion devices does not mean that the channel of distribution frowns on them. Manufacturers, when setting up sales promotion programs, view the devices basically as stimulating consumer reaction in the form of an increased volume of business. Retailers and wholesalers view a program in terms of how it affects them individually and what its benefit is, relative to the time and effort put into it.

Notes

1. Lewis K. Johnson, *Sales and Marketing Management*, Allyn and Bacon, Inc., Boston, 1957, pp. 537–538.

2. Robert V. Zacher, *Advertising Techniques and Management*, rev. ed., Richard D. Irwin, Inc., Homewood, Ill., 1967, p. 19.

3. Ralph S. Alexander and Thomas L. Berg, *Dynamic Management in Marketing*, Richard D. Irwin, Inc., Homewood, Ill., 1965, p. 385.

4. Fred M. Jones, *Introduction to Marketing Management*, Appleton-Century-Crofts, Inc., New York, 1964, p. 502.

5. Lee Adler, "Sales Promotion Effectiveness Can Be Measured," *Journal of Marketing*, vol. 27, October, 1963, pp. 69–70.

6. E. Jerome McCarthy, *Basic Marketing*, rev. ed., Richard D. Irwin, Inc., Homewood, Ill., 1964, pp. 646–647.

7. John B. Mathews, Jr., et al., *Marketing: An Introductory Analysis*, McGraw-Hill Book Company, New York, 1964, p. 412.

PART 2 / SALES PROMOTION DEVICES

The use of all forms of sales promotion devices is discussed in Part 2: two chapters dealing with consumer-product sales promotion devices, one with retail-store consumer sales promotion devices, and one with dealer and distributor sales promotion devices.

Some generalizations can be made about all kinds of sales promotion devices used to stimulate product movement. All products go through two stages of sales promotion: the introductory stage, relatively short but very critical; and, in the case of successful products, the much longer and more stable period of normal sales and profit. The study of product sales promotion is organized to permit the separate analysis of sales promotion devices that are used in either stage.

Introducing new products, even after thorough test marketing, is a hazardous venture at best. The product is most vulnerable to quality and production problems, and its advertising and marketing are usually still untested. However, at this time in the product's life, the greatest sales promotion demands are made. In most cases such a heavy expenditure in sales promotion will never again be tolerated or justified. Certain introductory mail couponing may cost $2 million, and a crew-delivery sampling may cost more than $5 million.

It is difficult to distinguish all kinds of introductory sales promotions for two reasons. First, some sales promotions that are used in new-product introductions are also adaptable to other purposes. Sales promotion devices of this kind have a dual capability. Price-off coupons are often used to encourage initial trial for a product but are also used to speed purchases of mature products. Second, there is not a standard method of marking the end of the introductory period and the beginning of the going period for a product. For present purposes, however, let us stipulate that the introductory period of a new product ends when the following three events take place (not necessarily simultaneously):

1. When a new product's share of the market reaches its first plateau, it is moving out of the introductory stage. This

may be true even if customers are in the market who have not tried the new product yet.

2. When a degree of distribution has been reached that is sufficient to support the first-level share of the market.

3. When consumer awareness and purchases of the product are sufficient to sustain that share of the market which covers the cost of the product and its distribution.

In Chapter 3, sampling, price-off coupons, and refund offers are described. Sales promotion devices of this nature are used mostly for products in the introductory stage.

Sales promotion devices better suited to the established, or going, stage of a product's distribution are described and analyzed in Chapter 4. Sales promotion devices of this nature are price-off promotions, premiums, and contests and sweepstakes.

In Chapter 5, those sales promotion devices which attract customers to a particular retail location rather than to buy a particular product or brand are discussed. Sales promotion devices of this nature are trading stamps, retailer coupons, dealer displays, and demonstrations.

Sales promotion devices used to sell the seller are covered in Chapter 6. They are dealer contests, money allowances, and retailer and wholesaler services offered by manufacturers. Sales promotion devices of this nature are used either to bring a product into the channel of distribution on introduction or to move it to a greater velocity if it is in the going stage.

The nature of sales promotion is such that it could be analyzed in many other ways, but it is felt that this analysis is the most profitable for both students and businessmen. Analysis of this nature treats of the use of sales promotion, as well as describing it.

CHAPTER 3 / INTRODUCTORY SALES PROMOTION DEVICES

Usually there are three kinds of sales promotion devices that are denoted as means of attempting to get consumers to try a new product. They are samples, price-off coupons, and refund offers. By the nature of each of these devices they are more suited to interesting consumers in trying a new product than are other devices.

The choice of a sales promotion device varies with the nature of the product, its market, and the competitive situation that it faces. These three factors affect the choice of sales promotion devices, and the generalizations here about the devices best suited to introductory-stage products are based on experience and logical assumptions.

Consumer sampling

Sampling as a sales promotion device is the actual offering of a free trial of a product to consumers.[1] The term is used in this narrow sense to avoid confusion with other marketing functions that are often referred to as useful in sampling consumers.

The word "sampling" describes the two identifying characteristics of this device. First, a trial size of the product to be sampled is offered to consumers. It is made available as practicalities and costs permit. It may be delivered to the doors of homes or apartment houses, or it may be offered for the taking in display bins in stores. Second, the offering of the product must be free to qualify under this commonly understood definition. In essence, sampling presents potential products to potential consumers for their trial and acceptance.

There are seven major objectives that can be accomplished through sampling:

1. Sampling induces consumer trial of a new or improved product, and this is the most important objective. Generally, if consumers do not try a new product, it is because

of their loyalty to another product or brand, their purchasing or shopping habits, or their unwillingness to risk a bad purchase. A free sample can change loyalty and habits and remove any financial risk from the trial. Less obvious than the possible advantages of sampling a new product are those of sampling an improved one. But an improved product may be, in effect, a new one. An improved product may be changed in taste, texture, color, weight, form, or even packaging or pricing to such a degree that a much larger market is open to it. A major improvement, particularly if it corrects a product disadvantage, may warrant a sampling operation.

2. Sampling builds a higher level of total volume for a brand by demonstrating and proving its superiority. Some products are so well established and have such loyal customers that only a free sample could obtain trial for a new and competitive product. Without sampling, even a worthwhile new product may not reach its potential.

3. Sampling is capable of building a higher level of volume faster than many other forms of sales promotion and often even outpaces advertising in accelerating consumer purchases. Sampling is immediate in action. Usually it is used in the first weeks of a product's life and speeds trial and acceptance (advertising usually produces this result only over a longer time-period.) One reason for the high rate of repetitiveness of an advertising message, or its frequency of impressions, is that the selling idea must be presented often to create the first image. Sampling, or free product trial, delivers immediate satisfaction and at the same time stimulates a first purchase. An exception to these generalizations is found in products that are health and beauty aids. Consumers may be so anxious to solve a personal problem that simply the promise of benefits prompts immediate purchase. New products that cure headaches, skin problems, dandruff, fungus infections, and the like, often draw such a rapid response, because the need is serious and personal. In the case of health and beauty aids sampling is not the means to promote products of this nature; instead manufacturers should use advertising or another sales promotion device that is more suitable to the buying practices of consumers of this kind of product.

4. Sampling attracts the fringe, or less likely prospects,

to a brand. Advertising or sales promotion devices like couponing tend to obtain trial only from primary prospects. A medicated soap is purchased and used mostly by people with skin problems. However, a free sample of such a soap may be used by members of a family who have no skin problems. If this product is also a good cosmetic soap, it may win many customers who ignore its medicinal qualities. Trial by secondary prospects is most likely under the conditions of availability that sampling provides.

5. Sampling encourages product trial even by prospects who have become disillusioned in a product category by repeated trial of other products that were unsatisfactory. Many products are marketed with less than a perfect promise of performance. Certain remedies cure or alleviate only a small percentage of the problems that they are bought and used for. Certain products for cooking involve complicated recipes and preparation, and results still depend on the cook. Hence, not infrequently, there is a widespread disappointment in certain kinds of products. Although it may be difficult to win consumer trial for another new product, even a superior one, when purchase of the product is required, a free sample may encourage such trial and convert a customer.

6. Sampling helps gain retail distribution for a product. Retailers know from experience that sampling is one of the strongest sales promotion devices and that it generates immediate product movement. Hence, they are generally cooperative in stocking a sampled product. This is not to say that other introductory incentives to the trade are not also necessary to gain distribution but only that sampling is one of the most accepted forms.

7. Sampling operates as an independent force. It can circumvent wholesalers and retailers. Sampling does not depend on advertising to deliver a message to prospects, nor does it depend on personal salesmanship or unusual retailer support. Sampling is the most direct channel of sales promotion for stimulating prospective consumers.

Counterbalancing the power of sampling are several negative factors and some pitfalls for the unwary user. As will be seen later, sampling is surely the most expensive of all sales promotions. Hence, an error in sampling carries a heavy penalty. It is, therefore, an essential part of intelligent merchandising to be alert to these dangers and to avoid costly mistakes. Let us turn, then, to the considerations that detract from the use of sampling.

Sampling is seldom, if ever, economically justified in the case of a well-established or mature product. In fact, the greater the share of the market that a product has, the less likely the opportunity for a payout on a sampling program. Because the mature product, and especially the mature product with a large share of the market, has been through the introductory or trial period, sampling at a later point reaches prospects who have already tested and accepted or rejected it. This duplication of sampling can hardly be productive of enough new volume to justify the cost.

It is doubtful that sampling wins a large number of new customers for a product that does not have an obvious and demonstrable advantage over its competition. Sampling is most effective for a product that is superior to its competition and can be shown to be so. This superiority may be in flavor, shape, convenience, or a number of other qualities. However, to sample a product without a reliable competitive advantage is only to convince prospects of its mediocrity.

Technological volatility creates a bad atmosphere for sampling. The risk and expense of sampling a product that is in danger of obsolescence are too great. This may not pertain to products in which marginal improvements are foreseen. However, if major developments are imminent, sampling should not be used. For example, it would have been unjustified to sample canned dog foods when the new dry dog foods were ready for the market, and, not much later, it would have been unwise to sample dry dog foods in the face of the even newer semimoist dog foods.

Personal-care products are not suited to broad-scale sampling. Shades of lipstick and perfume scents are quite individual in appeal, and so the selection is wide. The sparseness of prospects for a particular shade of nail polish renders its sampling uneconomical. Limited sampling, perhaps by a trained sales person and in a retail store, may be used, although it is quite expensive.

Items of slow turnover or narrow profit margin should almost never be sampled. The cost structure of such products tends to delay a profitable payout on sampling to a dangerously late date, perhaps for years in some cases. Herbs and spices are items that turn over too slowly to permit a reasonable payout period from sampling.

Some products cannot be sampled, simply because of problems of perishability, weight, bulk, or fragility. Products of this nature are simply eliminated from the possibility of sampling.

Certain products are purchased because of an unusual concept of their value rather than for their inherent qualities. Products of this nature do not benefit from sampling, simply because their inherent qualities are not outstanding or, perhaps, desirable. Some health foods are low in palatability but are purchased and consumed because they are "good for you." Sampling is not for these products so much as advertising or personal salesmanship.

There are also fine points to be considered in planning a sample, and they determine the practicality of a program or, more often, reduce a potentially mountainous cost to an acceptable level.

Seasonality of product use should be carefully traced and understood. Sampling should be accomplished in the season of peak use or in the period of increasing use before the peak. Suntan lotion may be effectively sampled in Florida in February but not in Minnesota before June. Less apparent examples of some degree of seasonality may be found in cake mixes, salad dressings, and other products.

Urban living has definite patterns which can be identified and which make sampling more selective and efficient. There are more dogs in the suburbs, more small families in city apartments, more young and growing families in new low-cost housing areas, and so on.

Sampling a new product too early in the marketing schedule is dangerous. Consumers must be exposed to sufficient advertising of the new product's brand name so that the sample has a value and is worth trying when it is received. A little patience in delivering samples may increase their consumption.

On some items that turn over quickly or on products that the trade traditionally holds in low inventory, sampling may create an out-of-stock condition at retail. The sample drop may win new customers so fast that they buy the product faster than retail shelves can be stocked. This problem may be compounded if the sampling and the first heavy burst of advertis-

ing are simultaneous. Test markets furnish information on the effect of sampling, so that this situation can be avoided or minimized in the major marketing thrust.

How large a sample must be distributed for a convincing demonstration is also a factor to be evaluated. Using a toothpaste once may demonstrate its pleasant taste, but it takes a long time to prove that it makes teeth whiter. Therefore, the size of a sample is relative to the product and its consumers' habits.

Sampling must clearly identify the product involved.

Usually, this can be accomplished by issuing the sample in a miniature of the full-size package. On page 42 is an illustration of the sample size of a product. A full-size package of a popular breakfast cereal is pictured with the miniature that was mailed during the introduction of the product.

In the main, these fine points relate to certain kinds of selectivity as ways of increasing the efficiency of sampling. Surely there must first be an analysis of how much product trial is worth and how much sampling will cost per case of product sold. There should also be a painstaking investigation of the various means and costs of delivering the samples.

This brings us to a discussion of the methods of sampling that are available to manufacturers. To be practical, this text is concerned only with sampling operations of a broad scope and with mass influence. There are too many kinds of sampling to be covered adequately here. Store demonstrators pass out samples of frankfurters or cake; cigarettes are given away with meals on many airline flights. These and similar sampling practices are quite specialized and limited. The concern here is with more extensive programs.

The more commonly used and successfully implemented kinds of sampling are described below.

Mail-delivered sampling is the most frequently used method. It permits economical and efficient coverage of sparsely settled areas and rapid coverage of heavily populated, urban areas. Mail delivery is especially suitable to lightweight or small-size samples.

Although speed of coverage and relative economy are this method's outstanding advantages, it is also true that most mailing houses today offer a high degree of selectivity in their lists. There are mailing lists of automobile owners, doctors, lawyers, and many other groups. Certain socioeconomic sections of census reports can be studied to increase the efficiency of the mailings. Further economy can be realized by feathering the sample—dropping it on alternate blocks, for example.

It is wise to check each sampling with the post office to be sure that the weight, size, and configuration of the package are within acceptable standards. The merchandise must also be permitted to be mailed.[2]

The factors of packaging and product characteristics determine the cost of the sample mailing as well as the number of units mailed. Sampling through the mails may cost from $1 million to $3 million. There are so many variables in the packaging of samples for mailing (size, weight, protection of product, and the like) that it is difficult to attempt a cost estimate. However, for an average product—a hair dressing or a bar of soap—mail distribution of samples normally runs from 4 cents to 7 cents per unit. Packaging and product costs must be added to the distribution cost to arrive at a total. The safest practice, however, is to discuss each sampling program with a reputable mailing house and obtain advice on costs and delivery methods.

Door-to-door sampling is another frequently used method. Samples are delivered by a specially trained and supervised crew. Door-to-door delivery is the most expensive and so is used only if technical problems prohibit less expensive means or if consumer use of the product is so great that mailings are impractical. Bulky or heavy samples can be distributed this way with efficiency in heavily populated areas. Even perishable products can be protected and controlled so that they are received in good condition.

Some precautions should be observed in planning a door-to-door sample drop. First, although trained and experienced crew supervisors are available from reliable mailing houses, it is best for the sampler to add some measure of on-the-job supervision of his own. With the exception of the largest cities, one or two experienced men can adequately represent the sampler in an overseeing capacity. The additional precaution helps the sampler be sure that the execution of the sampling is faithful to the plan. Second, it is safe to assume that crews are too expensive in extraurban and thinly populated areas. Third, sampling by crew is not a rapid method of distribution. Fourth, and to be attentive to a legal detail, crew-delivered samples are not permitted to be deposited in mail boxes.

There are two methods of door-to-door sampling of households. In the ring-and-leave method a sample is placed at the door, the doorbell is rung, and the crewman departs.

The ring-and-leave is the most commonly used method. A second and more expensive method is called ring-and-hand-in. The crewman rings the doorbell and waits a predetermined time for someone to come to the door. If the door is answered, the crewman hands in a sample and may deliver a sales message. If the door is not answered in a certain time, he leaves the sample and departs.

The counsel of a mailing house is also necessary for crew-sampling appraisals. Cost of labor, supervision, and packaging may vary widely. However, on the average, a sample can be delivered at a cost of 13 cents to 15 cents for the ring-and-leave method and 18 cents to 21 cents for ring-and-hand-in. Again, the costs of the product and packaging must be added to arrive at the total cost.

In-store sampling is a third method of delivering a product for trial. In-store sampling is an occasionally effective device but, more often, it fails to meet its objectives. One kind of in-store sampling, the passing out of samples by a demonstrator, has some legal as well as cost disadvantages and is not so broad in coverage as the more frequently used methods—door-to-door and mailing. Another kind of in-store sampling, worthy of some attention, consists of packing a quantity of free samples in a shipping case that opens up into a display unit. The display piece carries copy that encourages shoppers to pick up a sample. Because this kind of sampling incurs no postage or crew costs, it is quite economical, and wide distribution of samples is achieved inexpensively. Even if it is decided to pay retailers for display space, to pay them a special allowance for handling the free merchandise, or to compensate them for any loss of profit that they might have realized from the sale of competitive products, this kind of sampling is still inexpensive.

Because it is often inefficient, there are a number of negative factors also inherent in the help-yourself sample method. The first is the fact that retailers are subject to a great number of aggressive sales presentations aimed at capturing some of their limited special display space. Retailers are more likely to give this precious space to known profit producers than to risky new products. There is another problem—in-store sampling is extremely vulnerable to pilferage. There may be a high degree of pilferage by store employees out of the stock room or whatever space is used to maintain in-store inventories. Consumers, too, present a problem in pilferage, because they often pick up more free samples than displays suggest. A third disadvantage is that displays of free samples have a short life.[3]

It is difficult to estimate the cost of sampling of this nature. The costs of sample packages and of the product should be added to the cost of special shipping cases to arrive at a base cost. More care must be given to the matter of compensating the trade for profit on lost sales. There are no guidelines for this. Sometimes an allowance is given to the trade for each sample case displayed. Sometimes retailers are paid an allowance on the estimated profit loss caused by the retail unit sales captured by the free samples. Either way, to ensure retailer acceptance of the samples, careful judgment must be applied to set the money value of this handling allowance at a level that eliminates or minimizes loss of income to retailers.

On-package sampling is a fourth method. Sometimes a sample can be attached to or inserted in another package. As we have seen, when Aunt Jemima syrup was introduced, a sample was attached to Aunt Jemima pancake mix by means of a cardboard boot. Such natural product associations are not always present, but compatibility between the sample and its carrier should always be sought. This method offers low-cost distribution of samples and often obtains special display features of a sample of good value. In fact, the bulkiness or awkwardness of this kind of packaging is often unsuited to placement on regular shelves. In these instances, it may be necessary to process a simultaneous deal, perhaps a purchasing allowance, on the regular merchandise, so that there is on-shelf availability of the regular product.

This kind of introductory pack acts as a promotion for both products. The sample utilizes the branch franchise of the carrier to reach prospects, and the carrier itself benefits in that the sample is, in fact, a free premium or bonus.

The disadvantages of the on-package sampling method are several but not necessarily omnipresent. The special packaging may be expensive. It may even require hand packing in a boot. The breadth of sampling is mostly limited to regular buyers of the carrier product. The trade faces the annoyance of handling the special pack and, again, may need some compensation for loss of other sales.

An important warning. Free samples should be labeled so as to avoid their separation from the carriers for individual sales.

Isolated-group sampling is still another method. There are services that routinely deliver samples to identifiable and isolatable groups—brides, young mothers, and families who have moved.

Many products have special appeal for these groups, and members may be heavy consumers of the products involved. Baby lotion for young mothers is an obvious example.

The sampling of these isolated groups represents the ultimate in prospect selectivity, and usually participation in these plans is granted to a product on an exclusive basis. Prospects on these lists are at their readiest and are most receptive to new products aimed at their needs; the only waste results from the use of outdated and inaccurate mailing lists.

Costs can be obtained from special marketing-service organizations that specialize in sampling. Generally, the pitfalls in the isolated-group method of sampling are, first, the expense. Often the process of developing a highly selective list adds to the cost of the service. Second is the possible loss of control of the samples in the distribution, the uncertainty that they were actually delivered according to plan.

A final word on sampling should stress the necessity for testing. As expensive as testing is, even in less forbidding forms, sampling needs evalution in the field. One needs assurance and statistical measures of the proper amount of samples, the cost of the sampling program, and the ability of the sample to gain customers. Postsampling research helps determine a more selective base or measure the effect of sampling on brand awareness or even on the total marketing and creative advertising concept. Variations in result are so wide, and so frequently unpredictable, that the need for sensitive testing is demanded.

Couponing

In the broadest sense, many kinds of stamps and order blanks are called coupons.[4] Some such coupons may be redeemed by returning them to the manufacturer or taking them to a store or presenting them at a redemption center.

A coupon is a certificate that, when presented for redemption at a retail store, entiles the bearer to a stated saving on the purchase of a specific product. These certificates (coupons) are most often issued by manufacturers, sometimes by retailers, and infrequently by distributors and wholesalers. A. C. Nielsen Company, a coupon-redemption company, has estimated that more than 10 billion coupons were distributed in 1965.[5]

Coupons are, in effect, the same as money and are accepted as cash by retailers. The retailer, after taking the coupon in part payment of a purchase, later sends it to the manufacturer or his agent for reimbursement. The manufacturer adds a handling fee (usually 2 cents) for each coupon that the retailer redeems. The handling fee is to defray the retailer's cost of handling, sorting, and bookkeeping.

The basic strategy and mechanics of couponing are similar, no matter who issues the coupons. Because the greater quantity and variety of couponings are issued by manufacturers, it is from this standpoint that the importance of this popular device will be viewed.

The major capabilities of couponing are:

1. Coupons obtain consumer trial of a new or improved product. In the treatment of sampling, the powerful trial-inducing value of sampling was emphasized. If an equal number of homes are sampled and couponed, almost inevitably a higher degree of trial results from sampling. However, the coupon still induces a relatively high degree of trial and very probably creates more triers per dollar spent. Couponing is

not so strong as sampling but is by no means weak. Coupons can be used for increasing the use of a product or introducing a new product.

2. Couponing, like sampling, often builds a higher level of business than unaided advertising campaigns and does so more rapidly. A coupon is an action-getting device, because it is an in-the-hand bargain.

3. Couponing attracts the ripest prospects to a brand, those who most likely become repeat purchasers and regular users. The act of cutting a coupon out of a magazine or putting one in a purse signifies an intention to use it, probably based on some predisposition to try a product of this nature. People who like fish are more apt to redeem a coupon on a frozen halibut dinner than those who do not. Couponing can be used repetitively and even on established brands to deliver new volume and new customers for a long time. Coupons of different money value and delivered to consumers by different channels and with different selling messages continue to turn up new triers or to reconvert lost customers. Particularly in those categories in which product quality differences are indistinguishable, the bargain value of a coupon may cause a change in purchase habits.

4. Couponing sells new and larger sizes of a product. To introduce a new or larger size of a product, a manufacturer often uses a coupon. Such couponing may be inserted in the small-size package of the product or placed in magazines or newspapers. Although much of the coupon redemption may not be for the desired size of the product, the coupons will still be a definite and beneficial influence on the new item.

5. Couponing introduces a new flavor of a product or a variation. Certain product lines are variety-oriented. Cake mixes and snacks are two examples. To encourage the trial of flanker products within a brand line and to discourage trial of competitive varieties, coupons are most effective.

6. Couponing is also quite flexible and can be quickly activated. The preparation of sampling, for example, is a long and painstaking process. Couponing printing and mailing or even distribution through magazines or newspapers, can be quite rapid.

Having considered the plus side of coupon promotion, the prudent marketer should also examine the minus side. Although most coupons are redeemed within a few months of receipt, a long time may elapse before they are all collected. On almost any couponing, regardless of delivery method, the redemption rate reaches its highest point before 90 days after the drop. Redemption then gradually declines for five or six months, but a few coupons show up months, even years after issuance.

Coupons, inasmuch as they function like cash, are subject to fraud. Ways of minimizing the danger of fraud are limiting the distribution of the coupons to households, keeping their value down, and checking to see that their redemption does not exceed the amount of the goods sold. In addition to these problems there is also the threat of counterfeit printing or bulk redemption. There have been counterfeit coupon rings discovered and prosecuted within recent years.

Misredemption is another potential problem. Consumers and retailers occasionally apply coupons against the wrong product or even redeem them for cash. The problem of misredemption arises here and there, now and then. The problem is not universal, and an alert marketing group can spot geographical areas in which misredemption becomes burdensome and seek mutually advantageous solutions in cooperation with retailers.

Products that are purchased infrequently are not good candidates for couponing. The coupon will probably not drop on the prospect when the product is needed or about to be needed. Hence, the greater likelihood of either misredemption or a low level of redemption. A home permanent-wave kit is the kind of product whose rate of purchase is so slow that couponing is probably an impractical promotion.

Generally, the same fine points that can be interpreted and evaluated to increase the effectiveness of sampling also pertain to couponing. An analysis of them can determine the practicality of a couponing program or, even more important, reduce a potentially mountainous cost to an acceptable level.

Seasonability of product use should be carefully traced

and understood before starting a coupon program. Couponing should be done in the peak season of product use or in the period of increasing use before the peak. It would be proper to coupon picnic goods in the spring and summer.

Urban living has definite patterns that can be identified to make couponing more selective and efficient. Middle-class housewives in suburban areas are good prospects for coupons. Shopping is an important part of their lives, and coupons help them get value and economy in their purchasing.[6]

Couponing a product before it has an established brand name is dangerous. Consumers must be exposed to the product's name so that the coupon has a good value. If the product is not established as a value, then consumers are less likely to take the risk of purchase even with a coupon. A price-off coupon alone is not normally strong enough to give confidence to buyers.

Basic requirements for coupons Perhaps the first requirement for coupons, and this precedes a review of established practices and accepted formulas, is that a coupon should look like a coupon. As a commonly recognized medium of exchange, a coupon benefits from having a standard, certificate-like appearance. A coupon should be immediately recognized for what it is. Unusual design confuses consumers, inhibits a coupon's function, and reduces the redemption level.

As a substitute for money, or as a negotiable instrument, a coupon must meet certain rigid requirements. It must clearly communicate its nature to consumers. It should fit retailers' needs. It should give its issuer necessary legal protection. The following are the basic factors that one needs to observe in designing a coupon.

The nature of the offer must be clearly stated on the face of the coupon. This requires a statement that tells the money value of the coupon, the brand involved, the quantity and size of the product, and the place or means of redemption of the coupon. The value of the coupon is usually printed in large type in at least two places on the face.

The coupon must conform to standards that make it easy

★ STORE COUPON ★

FREE ONE CAN ANY VARIETY

Great American Soups

TOMATO VEGETABLE   CHICKEN RICE
CHICKEN NOODLE   VEGETABLE
VEGETABLE BEEF   CREAM OF MUSHROOM   CIS-4

Dealer: Send this coupon after redemption to H. J. Heinz Company, Box 4, Pittsburgh, Pa. 15230 for reimbursement of full price of one can plus 2¢ handling. Invoices proving purchase of sufficient stock of Great American Soups from Heinz to cover coupons presented must be shown upon request. Failure to do so will void all coupons. Coupon non-transferable, sales tax must be paid by consumer. Void wherever prohibited, taxed or restricted. Cash value: 1/20 cent. Any other use constitutes fraud. Good Only On Great American Soups from Heinz.   RHD   GS301B

Hearty Full Bodied Soup

Great American Soups

The Soup you don't dilute

for the retailer to handle it. It should be of one of two sizes:
dollar-bill or punch-card. The dollar-bill size is 2.5 inches
by 6 inches. The punch-card is 3.25 inches by 2.45 inches.
An illustration of each is shown on these pages. Perfora-
tions for a clean-cut edge are desirable but not required. Paper
stock of newsprint quality is acceptable but minimal for coupons. Coupons of these sizes can be accommodated by mechan-
ical counting devices and thus can be more easily handled.

RETAIL STORE COUPON FROM KIMBERLY-CLARK CORP.

7¢

7¢

Worth 7¢

on your
purchase of
new

KLeeNeX BoutiQue TiSSUes

Available in
pink, peacock,
gold or white.

7¢

This coupon good only on Kleenex Boutique tissues. Any other use is fraudulent.

Certain dos and don'ts must be observed in copy also.
Coupons generally have an expiration date, but they are
usually accepted for redemption after the expiration date to
promote good customer relations. It is better to have coupons
run over the time period, because manufacturers and retailers
do not want the sales promotion device to lose customers
rather than bring them in. The place and means of redemption should be clearly and prominently stated. The name of
the issuer is also necessary. The coupon should not require the
redeemer's signature. The retailer's handling charge, usually
2 cents per coupon, should also be noted, as well as any
special instructions regarding collections of coupons by the
manufacturer's sales force or by a coupon clearing house.

A few legal and protective requirements, although basic, must be fulfilled. Manufacturers may require retailers to purchase enough products to cover the coupons presented and void those presented without such purchases recorded. The coupon may state that it is redeemable only on a certain brand and reimbursement is only through authorized dealers. Some states require a cash value (usually $1/20$ cent) to be attached to the coupon.

An additional precaution is often observed by overprinting the word "void" on sample coupons used in sales-force presentations or in trade advertising.

Before presenting a description of each kind of couponing, a few words about determining the money value or face value of coupons are necessary. Generalizations may lead to error in determining the face value of coupons, and it is especially true that only testing and experience can help in learning the effects of varying face values of sales promotion devices. However, assuming that such testing is conducted, one can begin to calculate the face value of coupons within the limits of experience and certain guidelines. The face value of a coupon should not generally offer less than 20 percent or more than 35 percent off the retail price of a product if the coupon is to be redeemed at retail. On food and drug products the coupon should not allow less than 5 cents or more than 30 cents discount at retail. This does not refer to money-refund offers, which are usually redeemed through the mail rather than at a retail outlet.

Regarding the establishment of the face value of a coupon, one further remark may prove applicable. In planning coupon tests, it is well to note that certain rules of logic do not always apply. A 15-cent coupon does not necessarily draw a higher percentage of redemption than a 10-cent one, and an 8-cent coupon may draw as well as a 10-cent one. Judgment is no substitute for experience in determining the face value of coupons.

Methods of distribution for coupons Direct-mail couponing has certain strengths and capabilities not matched by other

methods of delivery. Direct mail provides maximum unduplicated coverage of households. It yields the best rate of redemption. It is selective of recipients and thus a highly effective
means of couponing especially in the area of cost per customer
reached. Also it can include several coupons in a mailing.

On the other hand, there are two important disadvantages to couponing through the mail. Direct-mail couponing is
more expensive than any other kind and, under certain cir-
cumstances, it is wasteful. It should be remembered that most
wastefulness is the result of inaccurate mailing lists. Reliable
mailing houses update most of their lists every 12 months,
and this should provide a good degree of accuracy for most
couponing. However, the accuracy of the list to be used should
be checked regularly by the issuer of the coupons.

Coupon mailing may involve a single coupon or several
coupons. The single-brand coupon is often printed as a de-
tachable (perforated) element of a mailing device. A single-
brand coupon is almost never mailed in an envelope, so that
the cost of stuffing can be avoided. An illustration of a self-
mailer on Tang is on pages 56–57.

Multibrand mailings are always stuffed in an envelope.
These coupons may all be issued by one manufacturer, with
each coupon redeemable against one of his products, or the
mailing may include coupons from several manufacturers.
These cooperative mailings are usually originated by a mailing house, and although a participant loses flexibility in
timing, he gains a considerable advantage in economy. The
first of these cooperative mailings was launched by the R. H.
Donnelly Company in the early 1950s.

Statistical data of the history of couponing are unusually
reliable and accurate. Even the percentage of redemption realized from a mail-delivered coupon is known. Specifically, on a
fast-moving food-store item of high consumer interest, the redemption rate of a mail-delivered coupon may approach 40
percent. On items that turn over more slowly or are of lower
consumer interest, the redemption rate may fall as low as 10
percent. The average rate is between 15 percent and 20
percent.[7] Coffee or milk thus draws more redemptions than
macaroni or baked beans.

Dear Friend:

Have you heard of General Foods' great new breakfast drink discovery—instant Tang? It takes the squeezing and unfreezing out of breakfast. Simply mix Tang with cold water—needs no refrigeration. You make it fresh by the glass or by the quart. What's more, Tang is richer in vitamins C and A than any orange juice, fresh, canned, or frozen.

This coupon is our way of acquainting you with Tang, or if you already use Tang it's our way of saying "Thanks". Won't you use it at your favorite grocery?

Cordially,

Frances Barton

Frances Barton

BULK RATE
U. S. POSTAGE
PAID
Chicago, Illinois
Permit No. 3298

To calculate the cost of a mail-delivered coupon program is an easy exercise in arithmetic. It is most helpful to verify the cost of distribution of the coupons with a mailing house and the redemption rate through costing and experience. For illu-

strative purposes, we assume a single-brand coupon mailing with a distribution cost of $50 per thousand and an estimated redemption rate of 20 percent of a total drop of 20 million coupons at 12 cents each (10-cent coupon plus 2-cent handling fee for retailers):

20,000 × $50	$1,000,000
4,000,000 redemption @ 12 cents each	480,000
Total cost	$1,480,000

The cost of distribution includes the postage, the cost of the mailing list, the printing cost of the coupon, and a profit for the mailing house. It should be remembered that most often, mail couponings are multibrand programs. The gross cost of the mailing increases in a group couponing, but the cost per brand decreases. Hence, three or four brands can usually be mailed at a per-thousand distribution cost ranging down to $20 or even $15 per brand.

Some major users of mail couponing combine another sales promotion with it.[8] This overlay promotion is intended to add interest, excitement, and customer involvement and thus increase consumer redemption and trade cooperation in retail features. Usually a sweepstakes is included in a mailed promotion package.

⌐The delivery of coupons in printed publications, or media couponing, is the most frequently used method of distribution. The important media for this kind of promotion are newspapers and magazines. In general, both these carriers offer the same advantages to issuers of coupons. The distribution (circulation of the newspaper or magazine) cost is low in relation to the total number of coupons distributed. Redemption levels are also low, and therefore the cost of redemption is low.

Although the selectivity of audiences in media couponing is not so available as in direct mail couponing, there is still a certain amount. The editorial policy of certain printed media makes this selectivity available. *Sports Illustrated* and *Mademoiselle* magazines are media that appeal to a certain kind of reader.

A final advantage of media couponing is that it can be activated quickly, particularly in newspapers.

The disadvantage of media couponing is inherent in the nature of newspapers and magazines. Retailers dislike coupons that are ragged and torn, because they are hard to handle and sort. Also, there is a high risk of fraud.

The last of the disadvantages of media couponing deserves special treatment, because there are several ways in which fraud can occur or redemptions become excessive. Some customers or even retailers have, on occasion, clipped coupons out of publications and presented an unusually large batch for redemption. Overredemption can be avoided by limiting the printing of the coupons to the home-delivered circulation of the publications. Naturally, this is only feasible for newspapers that have a strong home-delivered circulation.

In addition, the value of the coupon, particularly in newspapers, should not exceed the newsstand price of the paper. A 25-cent coupon in a 10-cent newspaper represents an invitation to mass misredemption. Care should be taken of the printing plates of the coupon so that they do not fall into unscrupulous hands. Also, coupons printed in strips invite misredemption, so that if several coupons are used in one advertisement, they should not be located side by side.

Within the category of media-delivered coupons, there are several different kinds of presentation. There is an on-page coupon in newspapers and magazines, and there is a pop-up insert coupon and a coupon in a gate-fold in magazines. Experience indicates the following differences in redemption rate for these three kinds of coupons when redeemed on a fast-moving product, such as a breakfast cereal:

TYPE OF COUPON	ESTIMATED REDEMPTION
On-page (newspaper)	2%– 5%
On-page (magazines)	2%– 7%
Gate-fold and pop-up (magazines)	7%–15%

Space rates in newspapers and magazines vary widely, and there are additional charges for unusual space units. In some cases, coupons can be perforated so that they present an even edge when torn out of the publication. The perforation helps in handling on automatic counters.

It is difficult to evaluate media couponing from the standpoint of both a food and drug manufacturer and a retailer. A coupon in a national magazine may be most helpful to the manufacturer but almost of negligible value to the retailer. For example, in a magazine of 7.5 million circulation a pop-up coupon may earn a 10 percent redemption. To the extent that this may mean 750,000 triers for a new product, the couponing may be quite efficient for the manufacturer. However, this number of coupons redeemed through all the food and drug stores in the country means only three or four sales per outlet—hardly a bonanza.

In-package couponing is another method of delivery in common usage. The coupon in this method is inserted in a package or printed on the label. The distribution cost of in-pack coupons is quite low, because the only cost incurred is printing and inserting the coupons. However, the rate of redemption is quite high. It also becomes, in effect, a promotion of both products involved, the carrier as well as the couponed product. In terms of the influence that the in-pack coupon has on the product, it has three important capabilities. It can be used to trade up consumers to a larger size of a product, and a strong brand can help a weaker one. In-pack coupons can also be used to help introduce a new package. Coupons distributed in the last of the old packages can encourage the purchase of the new ones.

Among the disadvantages of in-pack couponing are these. First, it is a narrow or limited offer. It can act only through the customers of the carrier product. Because a leading laundry detergent may have only 6 percent or 7 percent of the total market and a leading cereal only 9 percent, it is clear that this kind of couponing only infrequently achieves a high degree of reach. Next, retailers may reject in-pack couponing if they do not stock both brands, sizes, or flavors involved, and usually in-pack couponing is not a strong enough sales promotion device alone to obtain distribution on either product. Third, certain kinds of products (canned or packaged foods) and certain kinds of containers (lithographed cans) cannot carry a coupon. In this connection, it should be noted that in packaged foods only special nontoxic inks and papers can be used for coupons and there are several limitations to the graphic quality that can be achieved with present technology.

Probably, the most attractive feature of in-pack couponing is that it produces a high rate of redemption at a low cost of
distribution. However, the redemption percentage cannot be
predicted without test experience. Historically, the range of
redemption is wide. A coupon good for the next purchase of
the same brand may redeem from 25 percent to as high as
75 percent. A coupon good for the purchase of another
product, called a cross-ruff coupon, may produce from 10
percent to 40 percent redemption. Because the basic sales
velocity and consumer acceptability of both brands combine to
influence the rate of coupon redemption, only testing can
reveal a reliable percentage.

Other available techniques for distributing coupons are
so restricted or specialized that they should not receive attention here. For example, door-to-door couponing is almost always used in conjunction with door-to-door sampling. Mail-in
couponing, in which consumers mail in proof of purchase to
gain a price-off coupon, is quite weak and rather rare.

Money-refund offers

In money-refund offers, consumers are presented with a
proposition in which a sum of money is returned by mail to
participants who mail in a proof of purchase of a particular
product. Occasionally, the full purchase price is refunded.
Money-refund sales promotion devices may involve only one
product, as typified by the familiar theme, "We'll buy your
first package of XYZ product." On other occasions, these devices may involve several products, as observed in another
popular theme, "You buy the ABC product and we'll give you
the DEF product." Both these approaches are variations of the
money-refund concept.

The objectives of money-refund sales promotion devices
are found among the following. Trial of a product is among
the primary uses of such offers. As noted later, money-refund
offers are relatively weak and do not generate many redemptions. However, in combination with a high level of product
news value and advertising, they help introduce a new product. Money-refund offers also help encourage several product

purchases. Often several proofs of purchase of the same product or labels from several different products are required to earn a refund. One collects five front panels from a brand of frankfurters, sends the proof of purchase to the manufacturer, and receives a refund of $1.

Money-refund offers can be combined with trade incentives to obtain special displays of new products. In the introduction of frozen dinners in the 1950s, the Swanson Company made widespread use of a refund called the Silver Dollar offer. A silver dollar was sent to participants who mailed in two proofs of purchase. The excitement created by the new products combined with the money-refund offer helped the Swanson Company claim thousands of special retail displays for their frozen dinners. Money-refund offers can be employed, too, to help retailers tie in with other and more profitable merchandise. Such sales promotion devices as "You buy the ice cream and we'll buy the pie" or "You buy the cereal and we'll buy the milk" are the kind of money-refund offer that attempts to close several sales for the retailer.

Last, money-refund offers are a low-cost sales promotion device. Because consumers must purchase the products involved and mail in the proof of purchase together with a return address, there is a high degree of forgetfulness and therefore a low redemption rate. Because the highest cost in a money-refund offer is the actual redemption, the low redemption rate keeps the cost of the sales promotion device low.

In fact, the low redemption rate is the chief disadvantage of refund offers; it means that they have a limited influence on sales volume and only seldom can their effect be noted in factory shipments or share of the market. As a result, the trade recognizes refund offers as low in pulling power, and it is difficult to obtain retail cooperation for them.

An objective assessment of refund offers as a sales promotion device would probably classify them as somewhat stronger in certain product categories than in others. Refund offers must be considered least effective in categories of high volume and high promotion marketing—coffee and soap, for example. Refund offers may be somewhat more effective in categories of low sales promotion activity—ready-to-eat cereals and dairy products, for example.

An unusual attribute of refund offers is that users can exercise a high degree of control over redemptions. The addition or withholding of certain factors of the refund offer can dramatically increase or decrease redemptions. There are three factors that can be manipulated.

First, the value of the refund can be raised or lowered. On an item with a retail value of 50 cents there may be no sensitivity to an increase in the offer of 20 cents to 25 cents, but redemptions would rise markedly if the refund were raised to cover the full purchase price.

Second, the number of proofs of purchase can be raised or lowered. There is a direct relationship between the number of proofs of purchase and the redemption on a refund offer. A requirement of two labels reduces redemption by one-half over the requirement of one label, and a requirement of three labels reduces it to one-third.

Third, the method of promotion also raises or lowers the redemption rates. The more that advertising, publicity, or other sales promotion devices help the refund offer overcome forgetfulness, the higher the redemption rate. Although redemption rates are difficult to predict, the following percentages have some historical validity for a grocery-store item of average turnover: (1) If the refund offer is promoted only by magazines or newspapers, a redemption of 2 percent of total packout (product available at retail during promotion period) may be anticipated. (2) If, in addition to magazines and newspapers, the offer is promoted in point-of-purchase materials (tear-off pads, displays, shelf talkers, for example) the redemption may rise to 5 percent or 6 percent of packout. (3) Finally, if the refund offer is actually printed on the package, the redemption rate may rise to 12 percent of packout.

As to technical matters, the only decision in refund offers is whether the refund itself is made by cash or check. A general rule suggests that any amount up to 35 cents may be refunded in cash but that more than this amount calls for a check.

Perhaps the most critical area of decision in refund offers
is the recognition of their inherent weaknesses in relation to
the establishment of marketing and promotional objectives.
Realistically planned, money-refund offers are capable of
achieving only limited objectives. They should never be assigned a marketing goal of sizable proportions.

Notes

1. Otto Kleppner, *Advertising Procedure,* 5th ed., Prentice-Hall,
Inc., Englewood Cliffs, N.J., 1966, p. 421.

2. "P.O. Still Worries About 'Potentially Harmful' Mailings,"
Advertising Age, Dec. 5, 1966, p. 14.

3. Charles J. Dirksen and Arthur Kroger, *Advertising Principles
and Problems,* rev. ed., Richard D. Irwin, Inc., Homewood, Ill.,
1964, p. 528.

4. "Coupons: ANA Study Cites Dangers," *Printers' Ink,* May 18,
1963, pp. 25–28.

5. "Everybody's a Coupon Clipper Now," *Printers' Ink,* June 24,
1966, p. 3.

6. Janet L. Wolff, *What Makes Women Buy,* McGraw-Hill Book
Company, New York, 1958, pp. 239–240.

7. "Coupon Keepers Save $100,000,000, Bullion Reports," *Advertis-
ing Age,* Sept. 26, 1966, p. 162.

8. "Maxwell House, Corn Huskers Get Sweepstakes Drives," *Advertising Age,* Nov. 28, 1966, p. 27.
"Mailings have been delivering envelopes containing the following coupons: Warner-Lambert Pharmaceutical Co., for Corn
Huskers, 'the man's hand lotion,' a 6¢ off coupon, and information on a 'Match the Ingredients' Sweepstakes."

CHAPTER 4/SALES PROMOTION DEVICES TO INCREASE THE USE OF A PRODUCT

In the introduction to Part 2, the two marketing stages of a product, the introductory stage and the established stage, were noted, and in Chapter 3, sales promotion devices for introducing a new product or a product innovation were discussed. The present chapter examines those devices which increase the purchase of established products: price-off deals, premiums, and contests and sweepstakes. These devices are referred to as those which give an added value to consumers for the purchase of a product.

There are not any set rules for the use of sales promotion devices. Although price-off deals, premiums, and contests and sweepstakes are best used for established products, they may also be used for the introduction of new products or product innovations. Similarly, samples, coupons, and money-refund offers may also add value to products as well as being used to introduce new ones.

The reader should not assign a limited use to any sales promotion device but should remember that all sales promotion devices have secondary as well as primary functions in marketing. The primary and secondary functional analysis of sales promotion devices is based on a theory of marketing that anything that works is suitable to an attempt to increase productivity.

Price-off promotions

Price-off promotions are those sales devices which offer consumers a certain amount of money off the regular price of a product and flag the amount of the reduction on the label or the package. Sometimes these devices are called cents-off deals or price packs. Price-off promotions are the most controversial of all sales devices. They are sometimes attacked as price cutting and sometimes praised as a means of offering a legitimate bargain to consumers. Actually, a flagged price-off promotion represents the one sure way in which a manufacturer can process a temporary discount to the consumers. The flag carries with it the assurance that the bargain price is passed on to consumers and not retained by retailers.

Because price-off promotions receive almost constant criticism,[1] even from manufacturers who use them often, it may be helpful to study their advantages first. Price-off deals have five advantages that have made them the most frequently used sales promotion device.

First, price-off promotions are a strong trial-gaining device. A lower price is a sales stimulant in any business and so it can induce trial purchase and win customers from the competition.

Second, price-off promotions are often purchased in additional quantities by the trade—in anticipation of selling six or seven weeks' volume of coffee in four weeks, for example.

Third, partly because of the additional quantity purchased and because of their past success, price-off promotions often earn preferred and special display locations in stores.

Fourth, price-off promotions can help decrease a lag in sales of a particular size of a product. The large, jumbo, or small size can be promoted by a price-off deal.

Fifth, price-off promotions are highly controllable. The amount of discount, the amount of pack-out, the geographical areas to be covered, and the timing of the sales promotion can all be closely controlled.

On the other hand, there are serious disadvantages to price-off promotions. Some are traceable to the essence of any reduced price; others are created by the misuse or, more properly, the overuse of price-off as a sales promotion device. Most significant is the evidence that a high frequency of price-off promotions cheapens the image of a product. Some products are so frequently offered at a cents-off rate that they seem almost to have no regular retail price.[2] Price-off promotions are somewhat self-defeating in that they offer a price reduction to regular customers, many of whom are willing to purchase the product at the normal price. And price-off promotions often create only a short-lived sales increase. Usually, at the conclusion of a price-off promotion, a brand returns to its prepromotion sales level. The simplicity of price-off promotions encourages laziness in brand managers, who tend to use them even when the marketing situation calls for a more complex program. Finally, price-off promotions create problems for retailers. The merchandise in a price-off promotion may need special handling in the warehouse, so that it can be supplied as needed by the retailer, and then there is additional handling in the store. Some manufacturers offer a special handling allowance of a few cents a case to compensate retailers for the additional effort.

One of the more informative research studies [3] of price-off promotions was conducted on the basis of data collected by the *Chicago Tribune* Panel of Consumer Behavior, which gathered information about their strengths and weaknesses. The study covered 19 brands in three products—regular coffee, cleansing tissues, and frozen dinners. It covered a five-year period, 1958 to 1962, and intensive interviews and data searches were conducted in six manufacturing companies, two in each product class, to learn how price-off promotions were treated. Some of the highlights from the study are worth reprinting:

HOW DO SEASONS AFFECT PRICE DEALS?
The majority of annual price reductions occur in high-volume periods, but off-price deals are more effective in terms of both gains in market share and gains in absolute units, after accounting for differences in seasonal sales. Also, with total industry volume relatively lower, fewer regular customers will be taking free rides on the deal than during the higher-volume periods.

Off-season price reductions generally are of below-average magnitude, thus improving margins for the manufacturer. At the retail level, with fewer deals going at once, the trade has more freedom to be competitive, and quite likely the consumers are less confused than when there are myriad offers in a product class. Here are some pertinent specifics from the study:

There were 17 deals conducted by frozen-dinner manufacturers during the traditionally low-volume third quarter that resulted in gains 50% greater than those in the other quarters, and 11 of the 17 measured reductions were well below average in magnitude.

For cleansing tissues, off-season second and third quarter promotions were 2½ times as effective as those in the first and fourth quarters, and 17 out of 24 summer reductions were below average in magnitude. By contrast, 11 first-quarter reductions in shelf price resulted in a 0.7% loss in market share, on the average.

Most third-quarter (off-season) regular-coffee offers were below average in magnitude of incentive, yet were twice as effective as first- and fourth-quarter deals.

HOW DO THE FREQUENCY AND DURATION OF PRICE DEALS AFFECT RESULTS?

The closer together the deals for a brand, the poorer the results; that is, frequent price promotions by the same brand result in successively smaller gains, on the average. Indications are that the industry which relies less on deals of the consumer type has many more loyal customers for various major brands. Conversely, high rates of dealing (as in the regular-coffee industry) induce consumers to be extremely price conscious. In this study dealings were found to be a considerably less prominent feature in the marketing of tissues and frozen dinners than in the marketing of regular coffee; and reductions offered on the first two product types were of such smaller magnitude, but resulted in much larger gains in market share than did reduction on regular-coffee brands.

ARE PRICE PROMOTIONS EFFECTIVE IN COUNTERING COMPETITORS' NEW BRANDS?

Attempting to load the retailers so as to preclude their acceptance of an invading brand's offer is costly and largely futile. During such periods of high flux, dealing activity in the product class reaches a crescendo as well rooted brands fight a holding action against the invader; but the new entry ordinarily gains a foothold in spite of such maneuvers. To illustrate:

The steadily declining average price regular coffee reflected the stiff competition in 1958, but those were halcyon days compared with 1959, when all-out price warfare was precipitated by the invasion of Chico brand.* Chico coffee, initially advertised heavily in all media, accomplished about 90% sampling of metropolitan Chicago families, gave continuous

---

* All brand names are disguised.

trade allowances, and employed over twice as many salesmen as the major brand with the next largest sales force. All major coffee brands tried a delaying action during the first six months of the year, both before and after entry of Chico. Master Chef added to the chaos by initially trying a trade-loading combination of buying allowances and off-label consumer incentives. Retailers purchased only small quantities, however, reserving their favors for Chico.

After failure of its first move, Master Chef redoubled its efforts with an offer which trade sources said was of such a magnitude as to represent a marginal loss to the manufacturer. Another major contender, First Choice, elected to bide its time while the new brand expended its introductory resources. Significantly, that strategy enables First Choice to recover position quickly, and with a discount less than one-half that of Master Chef.

HOW ARE PRICE DEALS AFFECTED BY THE AGE OF THE BRAND?
Dealing is more effective for newer brands than for established ones. Generally the newer brands achieve high gains with relatively small price reductions, whereas older brands apparently find it necessary to offer larger concessions to attract new users and stimulate repurchasing. Likewise, the early effect of deal gains is more rapid for the older brands.

These notes from the "Strategy of Price Deals," cover, in brief, most of the basic considerations that one needs in assessing price-off promotions. However, these principles are not generally observed, and some product categories have degenerated into the practice of almost continuous price-off promotions. The instant-coffee business is an example. Fortunately, most users of price-off sales promotion devices have assumed a more conservative position. They have concluded that, in spite of the controversy, dangers, and weaknesses, price-off promotions earn acceptance and cooperation from retailers and increase product sales to thrifty homemakers.

Premiums

A premium is an item of merchandise that is offered at cost or at relatively low cost as a bonus to purchasers of a particular product.[4] Many premiums are offered free with the purchase of a product, many are sold through the mail for a reasonable price (25 cents, 50 cents) plus a box top, and a few cost many dollars ($5, $10) plus several box tops. Premium offers vary widely in intensity and effectiveness but not much in their objectives.

The objectives of a premium as a sales promotion device in almost every case are quite specific. The promoter of the premium anticipates that customers of competitive products will switch to his product because of the premium, discover the advantage of his product, and become regular customers or at least occasional customers. A premium can also be used to trade up consumers to larger sizes of a product. Premiums can be assembled into a long-range plan by means of a catalogue. The saving of stamps or coupons for premiums in the catalogue encourages repeat purchases and long-term customer loyalty. A premium may be made attractive to men by an offer of fishing lures or golf balls, and to women by an offer of dress patterns or artificial flowers for decorative purposes. Premiums also help add variety to a promotion that has become boring with only price-off or coupons.

In many modern corporations the development of premium planning and the selection of premium objectives is the responsibility of the brand manager and the premium department manager. Frequently, however, the responsibility for the premium itself is divided. Premium planning and selection are an extension of marketing planning and its objectives. Purchasing the premiums may actually be the responsibility of the purchasing department.

The purchasing of premiums may also involve their quality control, the reliability of suppliers, delivery, scheduling, and coordination with other technical services when necessary (packaging of on-pack premiums, for example).

The concern of sales promotion is mainly with premium planning and selection. Having noted the objectives that premium promotions can achieve, we examine the premiums themselves and the factors that influence their selection.

Selection of premiums A premium should be recognizable to consumers. No premium should be so inventive that it needs extensive explanation. In other words, a premium should not need its own introductory advertising program. A toy fire engine for children is a good premium, easily recognizable for what it is. Nylon hose, whistles, and watches need no lengthy description. A new combination knitting and crochet needle might need a lot of explaining, even for needlecraft experts, and so would be a poor premium.

A premium, however, may be unusual or a new or more attractive form of something familiar. Swiss clocks are an example, as are decorative cheese trays and carving implements.

Another commonly used premium is one which is utilitarian and which is presented for its bargain value. Hot pads, steak knives, and paring knives seem to appear regularly as premiums and often with success.

Things with a high degree of feminine appeal may be strong premiums, too. Imitation pearls, and even perfume, have been successful premiums.

In planning a premium sales promotion, one should always weigh carefully the value of the breadth of appeal of a premium against the possibility of aiming at a more selective market. At this point, it is best to return to the product's marketing plan and the objectives stated there.

The selection of a premium for a sales promotion is still quite an unsophisticated procedure in most companies that use them regularly. Premiums are usually chosen subjectively. In some progressive companies, however, premium testing programs and even premium market tests precede any large-scale or national promotion.[5]

Premiums may be tested in many ways. Some tests are conducted in the field or in stores. Several potential premiums may be tested at a time in perhaps three or four stores for each one. Records are kept of product movement before, during, and after placement of the premiums, and shelves are periodically checked to preserve as normal a buying situation as possible.

In another method, premiums may be pictured and described in leaflets that are mailed to known respondents to mail-in offers. Up to several thousand such mailings are made to obtain a sufficient number of returns for a degree of confidence in the preferences. A return of approximately 15 percent is necessary for the test to be sufficient.

A third testing method involves showing leaflets picturing and describing the premiums to consumers in their homes. Preferences are obtained in response to direct inquiry. Although this method is not always so informative as a vote taken by mail, because the number of respondents is considerably less, it can give a rough indication of preference.

There is one important caution to be observed in premium selection. As a matter of fact, the same caution applies to all sales promotion devices but especially to premiums. A release form should be obtained from everyone who submits ideas for premiums or sales promotions to a company. This signed form should give the company permission to use ideas without obligation. A sample form is not shown here, because there are so many satisfactory versions and each legal counsel prefers to select one and modify it for his company's need.

Kinds of premiums   There are four kinds of premiums, or at least four versions, used in sales promotion. Each is distinct but each also has something in common with the others.

In-pack or on-pack premiums are by far the most attractive. Because they are included with the product when purchased, they are an immediate award to consumers. No mailing or other effort is necessary to claim the bonus, for it is a part of the transaction. However, for maximum efficiency premiums of this kind become more effective as they become more visible.

Blister packs and shrink wraps are two kinds of packages made of plastic that offer high visibility. Lacking the opportunity to show the premium itself, one should make a good graphic presentation of it on the package that carries it. This kind of premium, as inexpensive as it usually is, can sometimes be strong enough to equal or even exceed in sales power a price-off promotion of equivalent cost. Free combs for adults and free whistles for children are among the classic examples of in-pack premiums.

Before subjecting possible in-pack premiums to testing and certainly before a manufacturer commits himself to one, each of the possibilities should be examined for feasibility. Does the premium give a noxious odor to the carrier product? Does it cut or damage the product or its package by sharp edges, weight, and the like? Is it the right size for the package and for automatic inserting equipment? Does its shape or weight necessitate changes in the shipping case, and how does this influence processing lines, conveyors, and the like?

The search for an in-pack premium requires care. Most often, in the food business, a user of in-pack premiums cannot afford to pay more than 10 cents or 12 cents for it. Inserting the premium or banding it to the package may cost another 1½ cents to 3 cents. In fact, on some small-margin products, one may not be able to pay more than 3½ cents to 4 cents for a premium. It is for this reason that so many plastic and paper premiums are on the market.

There are, then, really four things to consider: (1) appeal, (2) feasibility, (3) economy, and (4) durability. Artificial flowers, hairbrushes, steak knives, finger rings of plastic, dinnerware, towels—all products like these have been successful in-pack premiums. The painstaking task of searching for a promising on-pack or in-pack premium is worth the effort since this premium potentially is a very efficient sales promotion device.

The second premium to consider is really an in-pack premium, too. However, because it adds a further dimension to packaging, it requires separate mention. Reusable containers are among the strongest of premium sales promotion devices. The container or product package has the same value and immediacy as an in-pack premium. One finds refrigerated shrimp in a reusable dish or a large quantity of laundry detergent in a waste basket. The Kraft Cheese Company, for many years, sold processed cheeses in Swanky Swig glasses. Maxwell House instant coffee was sold in carafes with remarkable success.

Of course, reusable containers have the same advantages and disadvantages as any in-pack premium. However, they have an additional and unique advantage that, in one of two ways, justifies the additional cost. First, they replace regular product packages, and this packaging cost can be added to the basic premium cost to allow a higher price. Second, in many cases, reusable containers can be so attractive that the entire cost mechanics of the product can be escalated. A product that normally sells for 79 cents may sell faster at 89 cents or even $1.49 when offered in an attractive reusable package. The bonus is obvious, easy to understand, and, most important, at the fingertips of the consumer.

Free-in-the-mail premiums are the next in order of strength to attract consumers. In this offer, premiums are sent by return mail to consumers who send in a request for them and include a proof of purchase, such as a box top. Because this device requires use of the mails, it is considerably weaker than in-pack premiums. However, this limitation permits the use of premiums of a higher value. If in-pack premiums in the soap business cost an average of 3 or 4 cents, similar free-in-the-mail premiums cost an average of 20 or 25 cents (factory cost). The rate of redemption for free-in-the-mail premiums is lower, however, because of consumer forgetfulness or laziness.

Free-in-the-mail premiums introduce a new element, one pertaining to any premium except in-pack. This is the proof of purchase or multiple purchase. Two or three labels or box tops, rarely more, may be required to earn a premium. Care must be taken, of course, to maintain a reasonable proportion of the requirement of proof of purchase to the value of a premium. In fact, the redemption rate on free-in-the-mail premiums is quite unpredictable and resists reliable analysis even with testing. This has reduced their popularity.

Self-liquidating premiums are by far the most frequently used, because the cost of the sales promotion, including the cost of the premium itself, plus handling, packing, and postage, is recovered by the issuer. The issuer of the premium does not attempt to make a profit on the transaction, but he does try to avoid a loss. The key to successful use of self-liquidating premiums is the presentation to consumers of a premium at well below its normal retail price. The frequency of use of self-liquidating premiums can be traced, not to the strength of the offer to consumers, but to the low cost of the sales promotion device to manufacturers. Self-liquidating premiums may well be the most overused sales promotion device. They are recognized by the trade and consumers, as well as by manufacturers, as a low-pressure vehicle. A redemption rate of 2 percent of the offers that appear on retail shelves is usually the maximum.

Self-liquidating premiums are generally priced at $1 or less; 50 cents is probably the most usual price. It is advantageous to keep the price low so that more people can afford it. However, some self-liquidating premiums have gone as high as $5 or even $10, although they are rarely redeemed at a very high rate.

In the case of self-liquidating premiums the redemption rate of 2 percent is the most important consideration. Even on high-velocity items a redemption of 250,000 items is quite good. In products cased in 24s, this amounts to only about ten thousand cases, not much on a fast-moving brand.

A fair evaluation of this kind of promotion includes a mention of some of the more successful self-liquidators. Among these is the Texaco fire engine that was offered in 1964 and drew more than 1 million responses. In 1966 Pillsbury offered a paper dress, mad-mod cap, and matching go-go boots as premiums in a promotion for its line of cake mixes.[6]

One of the problems of self-liquidating premiums is that there has been a good deal of trouble in the field, mainly poor handling and administration. Premium handling should be considered a part of sales promotion, because, handled poorly, as many have been,[7] a premium can lose customers rather than gain them. This is a consideration in using self-liquidating premiums.

Consumer contests and sweepstakes

Similar in several ways, contests and sweepstakes are dramatically different in their influence on consumers and in their basic construction. Before defining contests and sweepstakes, let us clarify their position in the power scale of sales promotions, which are being considered here in descending order of consumer influence. In actual practice, this scale is not always a precise measure of effectiveness. This is especially true with contests and sweepstakes. For present purposes, let us roughly compare them with premiums. More specifically, a contest or sweepstakes tends to be as strong as the strongest premium offer (in-pack) and stronger than the weakest one (self-liquidating). In short, contests and sweepstakes are potentially a very powerful sales promotion device.

A contest is a sales promotion device in which the participants compete for a prize or prizes on the basis of their skill in fulfilling a certain requirement, usually analytical or creative. In a sweepstakes the participants merely submit their names to have them included in a drawing of prize winners.

Clearly, a contest requires more effort from an entrant than does a sweepstakes, and, as will be noted in the discussion of the legal aspects of these promotions, the additional effort required in a contest must be sufficiently sophisticated to permit a genuine demonstration of skill by the entrant. Hence, a contest does not usually attract so many entrants as a sweepstakes, but it does involve them more.

Objectives of contests and sweepstakes The marketing and merchandising objectives of contests and sweepstakes are the same, although they may vary a little in intensity. Contests and sweepstakes create a high level of consumer involvement in the advertising of a product. A famous contest from Borden asked entrants to name the new babies of Elsie the Cow. Other contests aim at new product uses, package identity, and the like.

Contests and sweepstakes can be developed to encourage action at the retail level, too. So-called lucky number sweepstakes require the inspection of a retail display to find the winning number. In addition to special display, newspaper features and special point-of-purchase material may be used to support contests and sweepstakes, especially if trade incentives are added. Contests and sweepstakes can help merchandise a television show right on the retail shelf, and a top-rated show or personality can be made into a fine in-store event.

Contests and sweepstakes add interest and excitement to a lagging product or advertising theme. They are strong overlay sales promotions. They are often, for example, superimposed on group coupon mailings to stimulate both redemption and retailer cooperation. They can be used to create major sales promotions on a group of products that singly would be limited to weak efforts. The combining of small individual budgets can create one large one.

The objectives, in effect, indicate the advantages of contests and sweepstakes, but as sales promotions they also have disadvantages. First, they cannot be tested. Some appeals and even prize structures can be compared with those of earlier contests and sweepstakes. However, no accurate, projectable market test is possible, if only because a large national prize list can hardly be duplicated at the local level.

Second, contests and sweepstakes alone are often not competitive enough to obtain in-store merchandising. In the mid-1960s, their number increased so rapidly that, unless they included other auxiliary sales promotion devices (price-off, special trade allowance), they were often ignored by an over-besieged trade.

Third, from the consumer standpoint, contests and sweepstakes have important negative characteristics. There are a great number of professional entrants who participate in all such promotions. They have, perhaps, a better opportunity of winning, and, more important, they can hardly be counted as loyal customers. These professionals, as well as others, often enter a contest or sweepstakes two or even more times. Although accurate figures on entry duplication are not publicly available, some experienced users of contests and sweepstakes fear that it is very common.

Fourth, it is difficult to ascertain the amount of media support needed for a successful contest or sweepstakes. There is a strong feeling that, particularly in the case of long prize structures or complicated themes, print advertising may be stronger than that of electronics media. However, because of the problem of testing, the feeling is not certain, nor is it a reliable indication of the amount of advertising needed.

Kinds of contests and sweepstakes   There are many kinds of contests—limerick contests, naming contests, estimating or guessing contests. There are also many kinds of prizes—money, merchandise, glamorous trips, and the like. A good analysis of all these possibilities is given in a report published by the Reuben H. Donnelly Corporation in 1964.[8] The many detailed records of contests and sweepstakes in their files indicated certain common elements in successful contest promotion. Unfortunately, these facts cannot be weighed or adjusted for kind and amount of media support given the promotions. The chart, then, on page 79 suggests trends but cannot be used to construct the perfect contest.

The key information that can be gleaned from the Donnelly report is that:

1. Sweepstakes have become more popular than contests.
2. Among contests, limerick and jingle completion types are more popular.
3. Among prizes, cash and choice of merchandise lead other items by a wide margin.
4. Cash prize structures of less than $10,000 in total are weak and unattractive.
5. There is a dramatic increase in appeal when the number of prizes offered exceeds 100.
6. There is little percentage difference between contests of $10,000 and over in prize structures, except for very large prize structures ($100,000 and over), which are highly preferred.

In the Donnelly report there is no way of measuring another element—and the most important—in the success of contests and sweepstakes as sales promotions. This element is imagination. Some contests have more appeal than others, because they offer a larger prize or a more alluring set of prizes. Even the entry vehicle, the skill element, may be inventive and attractive or even an enjoyable or fascinating task. Some contests have offered oil wells as prizes or new homes or trips to exotic places. Some contests use naming or the coloring of pictures or cartoons or a combination of naming and coloring to make the skill task more pleasant. Some sweepstakes are of the bingo type and others of the lucky number type in which a list of winning numbers is posted in retail outlets, there to be matched with serialized numbers distributed in the mail or through publications. These lucky numbers sweepstakes may fail, because many retailers do not cooperate in displaying the winning numbers. It is thus also true that many of the prizes offered will probably never be claimed.

THE DONNELLY STUDY

An analysis of hundreds of thousands of entries rates
effectiveness of contests components this way

	TOP CHOICE	SECOND	THIRD
Type	Sweepstakes	Limerick or jingle	Naming
Prize	Cash	Autos	Choice of merchandise
Value of prizes	$10,000 to $19,999	$20,000 to $34,999	$35,000 or more
Number of prizes	750 or more	350 to 749	200 to 349
Principal audience	General	Women	
Proof or task requirement	3 to 5 labels or proof of purchase	1 label or proof of purchase	2 labels or proof of purchase
Value of proof required	Less than 25¢	25¢ to 49¢	50¢ to 99¢
Length of contest period	6 to 8 weeks	10 to 16 weeks	Less than 4 weeks
Number of contest periods	5 to 6	7 to 9	10 plus
Contest opening date	February	April	October

Reprinted from *Incentive: Magazine of the Premium Industry*, January, 1965, p. 42.

There are several experienced and reputable business organizations that specialize in implementing contests and sweepstakes. They first appeared in answer to a need for independent and objective contest judging facilities. This service expanded, and they now help frame contests, obtain merchandise prizes, and give legal advice. Early consultation with these experts prevents serious miscalculations and delay in planning and execution of a contest or sweepstakes. In actual practice, it is the legal aspects that are the most confusing, and one should be aware of the following areas of legal danger.

Lotteries are illegal, and so no contest or sweepstakes should be a lottery.[9] There are three elements that must be present if a sales promotion device is to be legally construed as a lottery. First, there must be chance or luck. Second, a prize or prizes must be offered. Third, there must be consideration, a payment to participate in the lottery. If one of these elements is missing, the sales promotion is not a lottery.

Postal clearance should be obtained for all contests and sweepstakes. It may prevent serious embarrassment if the postal authorities construe a contest or sweepstakes to be a lottery, which would be illegal if sent through the mails, as well as being illegal under Federal and state statutes. Clearance may be obtained from the General Counsel, Mailability Division, Post Office Department, Washington, D.C. 20006.

In the matter of costs of a national contest or sweepstakes there are many important expenditures that must be estimated. Advertising-media expenditures may vary from a few thousand dollars to several hundred thousand dollars. The cost of point-of-purchase materials may also vary substantially. But advertising and point-of-purchase materials are the primary stimulant for entrants and need to be ample and attractive.

Prize structures may also vary widely but need some kind of advance budget commitment. Judging costs also vary according to the degree of difficulty that the judges might encounter in their work. In a simple sweepstakes, with no envelopes to be opened, judging costs start as low as $4 per thousand with a minimum fee of $500. Costs rise as more labor is added or more judging discrimination is required.

One of the thorniest problems with contests and sweepstakes is the postpromotion evaluation of results. Sometimes contests that draw as few as 100,000 entries may be more successful than those that draw 1,000,000. Often the real objectives of a contest or sweepstakes are best established on the basis of obtaining special displays, additional shelf facings, additional cases of product sold, sensitivity of response to product-advertising-oriented contests, increase in the share of the market, and the like. In essence, this means that the basis for evaluation should be clearly stated in advance so that unreal or misleading measurements are not arbitrarily applied later.

Notes

1. "Federal Trade Commission Gets Tough on Cents-off ' Promotions," *Sales Management,* Nov. 15, 1966, p. 112.

2. "FTC Plans New Crackdown on Coffee Deals," *Advertising Age,* Oct. 31, 1966, pp. 1, 7–8.

   "The FTC announcement said reports and hearings since it began studying the problem last January show that 'cents-off' sales, bonus packs, and other deals are all part of a variety of sales tactics which may mislead the public.

   "With respect to some brands of coffee, one or more of these offers have been so frequent and so long continued that the bargain represented may be in fact non-existent, FTC said.

   "It is clear that any purported savings claims must be based upon the actual bona fide price at which the article was offered to the public on a regular basis for a reasonably substantial period of time."

3. Charles L. Hinkle, "The Strategy of Price Deals," *Harvard Business Review,* July–August, 1965, pp. 75–85.

4. George Christopoulous, "Premiums: Growing Power behind Today's Selling," *Management Review,* vol. 38, no. 5, p. 9, May, 1959.

5. "Incentives: Selling's Mighty Motivators," *Sales Management,* Sept. 10, 1966, pp. 90ff.

6. "Pillsbury Offers Paper Dress, Boots, Cap to Boost Mixes," *Advertising Age,* Oct. 24, 1966, p. 8.

7. "FC&B Studies Premiums, Finds 'Such Poor Handling It May Lose Customers,'" *Advertising Age,* Dec. 24, 1966, p. 94.

8. "The Donnelly Study," *Incentive: Magazine of the Premium Industry,* January, 1965, pp. 1–14.

9. Marshall Howard, *Legal Aspects of Marketing,* McGraw-Hill Book Company, New York, 1964, p. 141.

CHAPTER 5/RETAIL STORE SALES PROMOTION DEVICES

In Chapters 3 and 4 sales promotion devices that attract consumers to the product of a manufacturer were discussed. In the present chapter, those which attract them to stores or influence them to buy a product at retail are presented.

Sales promotion devices aimed at affecting consumers at retail are important in the volume of business for both manufacturers and wholesalers as well as retailers. Devices that attract consumers to a particular store, such as trading stamps and retailer coupons, help build consumer loyalty to the store as well as increase the volume of business for the retailer, and any increase in sales at retail also affects suppliers.

Retail sales promotional devices, such as point-of-purchase displays or demonstrations of products, also work with consumer sales promotion devices and advertising, because they remind and restimulate consumers to purchase. Good sales promotions at the retail level are as important as any other sales promotion device used in business today.

The basic problem with all retail sales promotion devices is that, if a device is to function properly, retail management must cooperate in the promotion. This cooperation normally includes allocating space and handling the promotion. But retail management often does not cooperate, and this indicates an overexposure to sales promotion devices or a lack of communication with the manufacturer offering the sales promotion device. The problem with retail sales promotions is found as often in retail management as in the device itself.

All retail sales promotion devices, like the consumer sales promotion devices discussed earlier, are important to total marketing strategy. Each retail sales promotion device has its role, and each must be analyzed so that it can be used as effectively as possible. Sales, or rather more profitable sales, is the prime goal of retail sales promotion.

Trading stamps

Trading stamps are a form of premium in that they are given for purchasing or rather for purchases in a particular retail location. The number and value of stamps that the buyer receives depends on the value of the purchase.

Trading stamps are saved by consumers and then redeemed for merchandise. The consumers receive trading stamps in proportion to the dollar amount of goods purchased. The stamps are then redeemed either through premium catalogs or through redemption centers that stamp companies set up.[1]

The widespread use of trading stamps as a sales promotion device developed after World War II, but the trading stamp itself is more than two-thirds of a century old. The early stamp programs were of low volume and were used in regional areas exclusively.[2] Trading stamps seemed to appear on the American retail scene in numbers with the advent of self-service at retail stores and increased emphasis on one-stop shopping, and both these innovations in retailing occurred after World War II. This is not to say that there is a cause-and-effect relationship between trading stamps and self-service and one-stop shopping at retail but that they developed at the same time.

The trading-stamp business in 1965 reached a volume of $700 million in stamp sales—big business and an important sales promotion device. In fact, about 85 percent of all households in the United States save trading stamps, and more than 50 percent save more than one kind. Trading stamps are used by many kinds of retailers, such as gasoline stations, department stores, food and grocery stores, drugstores, and dry cleaners.

There are stamp plans for individual products or brands, such as cigarettes, but trading stamps that include a number of products are usually more successful. Homemakers seem to appreciate the opportunity to collect a large number of stamps in a short time. Stamp collecting gives the housewife the opportunity to redeem the stamps for a premium and see the tangible benefits of her savings. Housewives view trading stamps as a premium for purchasing rather than as a cost. In this way they can accept the stamps and claim the premiums without feeling guilty.

Trading-stamp plans have become highly controversial. Some retailers consider their use the most important and positive element in the retail marketing program; others consider them wasteful and exhorbitant. In the food business, experts estimate the cost of trading stamps between $2\frac{1}{2}$ and 3 percent on each dollar of retail sales. Trading-stamp costs are even higher in other businesses. Trading-stamp plans have survived, however, and in many cases have proved their worth in gaining and holding customers. Conversely, retailers who have dropped trading stamps or who have never used them but have substituted a program of low prices have also been successful. Neither the use nor the lack of a trading-stamp program means success in a retail business. Whether to use a trading-stamp program or not seems to depend on business conditions, competition, and the nature of a particular business.

The mechanics of the trading-stamp plan are simple. A trading-stamp company, such as McDonald or S & H (Sperry and Hutchinson), sells trading stamps to retailers, usually only to one store in each kind of business in each community, although to retailers in as many kinds of business as possible in each retail area. The retailers pay 2 to 3 percent of their average sales,[3] and they give the stamps to their customers, usually one stamp for every 10 cents of purchase. The customers save their trading stamps in books supplied by the trading-stamp company through the retailer and redeem them for merchandise premiums either through the catalog or at premium redemption centers operated by the trading-stamp company.

The retailer benefits from the use of trading stamps by an increase in volume of business or possibly of business that would otherwise be lost to competitors. The benefits that he receives will only be illusory, however, unless his use of trading stamps increases his volume enough so that their cost can be spread over a broad sales base. In the case of the 3 percent charge for the trading stamps the increase in volume would have to be maintained. by increasing either prices or volume so that the added income would cover the cost of the stamps.[4]

Trading stamps are not generally used by retailers who handle high-margin merchandise, high-price goods, or intensive service commodities but by those whose products are of low margin or are convenience or shopping goods. Such retailers are normally in a highly competitive situation where volume is the basis of their business. Trading stamps have generally been used most successfully by food and grocery stores, gasoline stations, and the like. Appliance dealers and sellers of men's and women's ready-to-wear do not normally give trading stamps.

Another factor that affects the use of trading stamps is the nature of the competition. The Great Atlantic and Pacific Tea Company's decision to use them in their retail grocery chain a few years ago was the result of competition. Although they could have given them before, they had not up to that time. The competitive climate changed and A & P elected to meet competition by adding trading stamps to their promotional program. This was a major change in the A & P policy and merchandising philosophy.

Trading-stamp-company operation   Trading-stamp companies sell trading stamps to retailers and then redeem them from consumers. They get their revenue from four sources. A modest profit is made on printing and selling stamps. The second source of income is from those stamps which are not redeemed (they are lost or destroyed). The third source of income is from the float, the time lag between the purchase of the trading stamps by retailers and their redemption by consumers. During this time the company holds the money paid by retailers in anticipation of at least a 95 percent redemption and earns interest on it—at least the prime rate and perhaps a little more. The fourth source of income is from the markup taken on the premiums sold through redemptions. The following illustration will help make this clear.

A trading-stamp company buys an item at wholesale because of the volume of the purchase. In setting the redemption value for the stamps, the company uses the average retail price of the item. For example, a stamp company buys a lamp for $4 at wholesale. It establishes the redemption value at three books, which is roughly $9 at retail. This markup on the redemption of goods gives the trading-stamp company an additional source of income.

Trading-stamp programs seem to appeal particularly to women. They seem to them to be good management and offer them an opportunity to save for something which is needed in the home but which they would not buy out of their expendable income. As long as this attitude exists, trading stamps will probably be an important sales promotion device.

There is another aspect to trading stamps that should be mentioned. Once a trading-stamp program is put into operation by a retailer, a certain number of his customers will shop there because of the stamps. If he discontinues the program, he will alienate this portion of his clientele. He may compensate by installing price promotions, but he dare not drop promotions entirely.

A word of caution is necessary here. Trading stamps must not increase the price of goods at retail so that customers are paying additional money for their purchases when they get stamps. Nor must the stamp program be promoted so that the consumers or retailers believe that stamp plans do raise the price, even though it is not raised. Some recent observations at retail have shown that, if prices are raised or if the consumers have felt that they have been raised, the consumers would rebel by not buying at those retailers. The retail boycotts by customers in the fall of 1966 were partly caused by their belief that prices had been raised to pay for trading stamps.

There have been moves by various groups to have trading-stamp plans outlawed in some states. Although there has not yet been any legislation so drastic as to eliminate the plans entirely, there has been some that has affected the stamps. The stamps must be redeemable in cash if a consumer so desires, and the true value of the stamp must be shown on its face.

Also, there has been a cyclical pattern in the impact of trading stamps that has been partly caused by a loss of enthusiasm for saving stamps at times and an increase in enthusiasm at others. Consumers are mostly affected by the current fad, which is now contests and sweepstakes. Retailers are also affected by the cyclical pattern in consumer preference for stamps, but trading stamps have generally shown a steady long-term growth that seems to be continuing as the peaks and valleys of short-term cyclical fluctuation even out over a longer time.

Retailer coupons

Not a recent innovation in retail sales promotion but one that has blossomed to an extent in the last few years is retailer coupons. Many of the benefits derived from national manufacturer coupons are also derived from retailer coupons, but their purposes are somewhat different.

Retailer coupons differ from those of national manufacturers in that they are distributed for a kind of product as well as for a particular brand. Retailer coupons are good for 10 cents off a half-gallon of ice cream or a particular brand of ice cream. Retailer coupons build volume, as well as selling a particular brand.

Retailer coupons are usually given on a number of products of the consumer-goods class, that is, those products which the consumer buys when price is an important reason for purchasing at that time. Retailer coupons can attract consumers to buy individual brands and can stimulate purchase of these items. The price-off feature of retailer coupons tends to stimulate and increase movement of those brands couponed for an individual retailer.

Retailer coupons are usually distributed in retailer's ads in newspapers or in throwaways that he distributes to consumers in his shopping area. Both newspaper advertising and throwaways are inexpensive, and because of the low cost of the means of distribution and the minimum investment, retailers like to use coupons. In fact in many cases they prefer their own rather than the manufacturers' because their cost is low and their effectiveness high.

Retailers feel that they get better results with their own coupons rather than manufacturers' in many cases because consumers are not limited to a particular brand but can use the coupons for any brand that a retailer carries. Moreover retailer coupons make consumers buy goods at a particular store, and they tend to do most of their shopping in the store where they are redeeming coupons.

There are two problems associated with retailer coupons. First, as their use becomes highly competitive, they lose their effectiveness somewhat. Retailer coupons tend to bring consumers to stores to use the coupons for those goods which they want, but then the same consumers go to other stores to use the coupons of competitors for other products. In this situation retailer coupons may become defensive, and their use does not tend to build traffic and volume for a retailer, who must then find another way in which to attract consumers.

Another word of caution is necessary here. If retailer coupons become defensive, it may not be possible to discontinue them, although a retailer wishes to. Because of the competitive aspect to retailer coupons and their impact on consumers, a retailer may be forced to keep them, just as he may be forced to start a coupon program to keep customers or maintain a level of sales.

Second, a retail coupon is really nothing more than a price reduction on those items on which a retailer gives a coupon. Price cutting, by using coupons or in any other form, does not tend to develop loyalty to a retailer but rather tends to develop in consumers the practice of shopping for the best price for each item. Retailer coupons would then seem to be doing a disservice to retailers who use them because they tend to become a price-shopping venture for consumers who redeem them. If a retailer is attempting to build loyalty to his establishment, then coupons may not help. If he is simply attempting to build traffic for a limited number of commodities, then coupons may be a highly successful means of doing so.

Retailer coupons are more important for some kinds of stores than for other classes of retailers. Retailer coupons are practical only for low-price items of high volume. They are normally used by grocery chains, variety stores, and discount houses. For example, an item priced over $2 would not normally be a suitable product for retail coupons, because the coupon must represent a distinct price-off. Five cents off a pound of coffee priced at 80 cents would be more suitable. Ten cents off an item priced at $2 would not normally be a large enough price cut to attract consumers.

Retailer coupons have been most successfully used in the retail grocery field, which offers high-volume, national brands and consumer self-service. Retail groceries have used coupons to increase traffic and volume of business, as well as to compete with other sales promotion devices and in other situations. One important factor is that coupons, like trading stamps, should not raise the prices in the stores nor should they reflect that prices might have been raised to pay for the coupons.

Retail display

The displays used in retail stores are called either point-of-purchase (POP) or point-of-sale (POS), depending on one's viewpoint. The purpose of all retail display is to make customers purchase the goods exhibited.

There has never been much discussion by marketing men about the function of retail display. Does it act simply as a reminder to consumers of their need or desire for a product? Does it stimulate them to buy a product for itself? Does it reinforce other forms of sales promotion to which they have been exposed, or does it stimulate the so-called impulse purchase?

There has not been enough market research on retail display, and so it cannot be affirmed or denied that a particular retail display stimulates any or all of these motivating forces. The important point is that retail display reaches consumers when they are buying, that is, when they are actually spending their money.[5]

Kinds of retail displays   There are many kinds of retail displays, and some of the most common are discussed here. Outside signs are one of the most important forms of point-of-purchase or point-of-sale. They are the large product or location identification pieces used to tell consumers that a retailer handles a brand or line of merchandise. They have been used extensively for many years by soft drink and tobacco companies.

Other companies now furnish retailers with outside-store identification signs that incorporate the brand name of the company along with the name of the retailer. Such displays are
used for gasoline service stations, paint stores, and fran-
chised appliance dealers.

Another form of retail display that attracts attention and
brings consumers into a store is window display. The windows
of stores have been used extensively for many years as a retail
display. The effectiveness of window display is greatly en-
hanced when a window is used to answer the questions that
consumers may have about the products shown there. Window
display should not only show the products that a retailer
carries but how they can be used and the accessories that can
be used with them. Store windows have been used most effectively by department stores and women's and men's ready-to-
wear stores particularly.

Counter pieces are another form of retail display. They
range from small, simple merchandise display cases placed on
top of a retail counter to complete showcases built by manufacturers especially for retailers.

Also included in counter pieces are reprints of print
advertisements mounted on cardboard and placed either on the
counter or in the store windows. Counter pieces can be open-
faced, merchandise self-selectors as well as enclosed cases. They
are most often used at the checkout counters of supermarkets
or other retailers that are primarily self-service, and they are
most frequently effective for impulse goods.

Display racks and self-service cartons are another form of
retail display. Racks, usually of wire or metal, are designed to
hold the merchandise being displayed. They may be counter-
racks, side-wall racks, or end-of-the-counter racks. The most
important aspect of display racks is that they actually hold
and show the product being displayed. Similar to racks are
shipping cartons that fold out into self-service display pieces.
The carton actually becomes a display piece for the merchandise inside, and it is normally designed to fit the end of a
counter or special locations in stores.

Racks and other self-service display pieces are normally
used by supermarkets, drugstores, and other retailers that pri-

marily carry self-service products. Impulse products are especially suited to racks or fold-out cartons.

Also included in retail displays are shelf strips, shelf talkers, overhead banners, and any of the attachments placed on counters or shelves. These forms of retail display help consumers identify products or direct them to the products being promoted by these devices.

Purposes of retail display   Manufacturers use point-of-purchase devices as part of the total marketing effort. The purpose of these displays, like all forms of sales promotion, is to increase the sale of a manufacturer's products. But manufacturers particularly wish the retail display form of sales promotion to remind consumers at the retail level of their products as well as identify them for the consumer.

Second, and perhaps as important, the purpose of point-of-purchase displays is to stimulate impulse buying—purchasing in which the decision to buy, or at least the choice of a brand, is made in a store. The better the retail display and the better its position in a store, the more likely it is that consumers will see it and buy the product.

The third purpose of point-of-purchase display is to influence retailers to take on a product. In retailing today, shelf space is one of the most valuable commodities. Displays at point-of-purchase are used to influence retailers to allot some of this valuable space to a manufacturer and to show his product. Good construction as well as attractive design is also an important factor.

One of the most important considerations in constructing point-of-purchase displays is whether they will be effective or not. Will they maintain, at the retail level, the manufacturer's message and brand image as created by his advertising and other sales promotion activities? Will they stimulate impulse buying as well as remind consumers? Will they make retailers carry more of a manufacturer's products and merchandise them better?

Factors to be considered in designing retail displays   If retail displays are to perform the marketing function for which they are intended, then a number of factors should be considered in designing and building them.[6] First, they must be attractive and must suit the structure and decor of the store as well as compete with other displays. They must be attractive enough to catch the eye and bring consumers to this product rather than to the competition. And they should be strong enough for product identification.

Second, the materials used in their construction should be of such a nature as to build the confidence of consumers in the value of the product. If consumers value the product, it will help them overcome their fear of the risk involved in its purchase.

Third, they should give information about the product so that consumers can make up their mind whether to buy it or not. The information must be concise enough so that it can be recognized and understood at a glance, but it must also be explicit enough to tell consumers what the product can do and how it can be used.

Fourth, they should create the proper atmosphere for the product. The point-of-purchase material must be appropriate to the retail establishment, and the display must place the product in an atmosphere of attractiveness and utility.

Fifth, they should attempt to give the impression that the product is valuable and is worth the price. Quality in goods is measured by consumers in value and worth, and it is important that retail displays communicate these attributes if they are to influence consumer purchase.

Sixth, they must be attractive enough to gain a preferred position in the store. In the competition for space at retail, the emphasis of displays must be on economy of space and efficiency of operation for retailers, but displays must also maintain their attractiveness.

Problems of retail display   Regardless of the value or beauty of retail displays, manufacturers will never be able to stimulate and motivate consumers unless retailers are willing to display material supplied by manufacturers. Because retailers have limited space, they tend to use it for merchandise or storage rather than for display. The better the point-of-purchase piece is designed to accommodate product display and storage, the greater the chance that retailers will use it.

As more and more merchandise comes into the marketplace, not only in new products, but also in different brands of similar products, more point-of-purchase displays will also be forthcoming. Stores cannot get much larger; and so the competition for display space will increase, and this will create more problems in the handling and use of point-of-purchase materials.

The lack of space at stores has made it extremely difficult for manufacturers to have their point-of-purchase displays used. Most retailers are not against product display or facings, but they do not wish to give up valuable product space for display pieces that do not actually show the product to a maximum. A point-of-purchase display that primarily shows a product and is designed as a self-starter has a good chance of being used by self-service retailers.

Another problem in the use of point-of-purchase displays is that some of them are not suited to many retailers. They are too large to handle easily, they are difficult to assemble, or they are made of such poor materials that they cannot stand the normal wear and tear of retail traffic.

A few pointers for manufacturers that may help them in planning point-of-purchase displays so as to ensure that they have a better chance of being used at stores are discussed here. Many point-of-purchase displays are so poorly constructed that they are worthless to retailers. The material used in their construction is of such a poor quality that they tend to be quickly destroyed by retail traffic and retailers will not use them, or if they do, the displays do not last for the period for which the sales promotion was designed. Moreover, poor materials and construction of retail displays make the product displayed look cheap.

Because of the number of displays being distributed and the amount of merchandise that retailers are handling, there must be better communication between manufacturers and retailers. Manufacturers cannot expect retailers to use every display that they receive, but there are cases in which a point-of-purchase display was not used by a retailer because he did not know about it.

One of the most commonly unused point-of-purchase displays is the fold-out shipping carton. In some cases a stock clerk tears off the top of the carton and puts the merchandise on shelves. The reason for the nonuse of fold-out cartons is normally that a retailer did not know that the display was a part of the shipping carton.

Better communication must also be developed between manufacturers and retailers concerning special offers relating to point-of-purchase materials. If a manufacturer is offering a money allowance to retailers for displaying certain merchandise, this must be communicated to all the retailers who may be eligible (this is not only a trade problem but also a legal one). Because of the dual nature of money allowances to retailers, they must be told what the terms of the allowance are, who is eligible to receive it, and how to collect it. Retailers must also be told how to substantiate performance of the terms of the deal.

The difficulty of measuring the effectiveness of point-of-purchase displays adequately leads to many problems for both manufacturers and retailers. The basis for measuring the effectiveness of point-of-purchase displays has been retail traffic. The more people who pass through a store, the more business the store can expect. Retail displays of all kinds are supposed to increase the traffic flow, remind consumers of needs and desires, and create impulse buying. The theory is sound, but what of the actuality?

Analysis by traffic means nothing more than counting the people who pass through a retail location. Although traffic measurement has been specialized to a degree by dividing consumers into their socioeconomic groups by age, sex, location of home, and income, it does not help analyze the effectiveness of displays.

Some manufacturers and retailers depend on retail store audits to show how well a product with a point-of-purchase display did in comparison with the competition. Also, retail audits can be used to show the change in the movement of goods for a period of time when there was a display compared with a similar period when there was not. However, retail store audits show nothing more than the movement of goods. They do not show the effectiveness of a display, because they cannot measure the cause-and-effect relationship between a display and the movement of goods.

What is needed is more research on the effectiveness of point-of-purchase displays, their value in increasing consumer interest, and their importance to both retailers and manufacturers.

Finally, the method of distribution of point-of-purchase displays is something for manufacturers to consider. There are usually five ways in which displays can be distributed to retailers: [7] (1) by manufacturers' salesmen, (2) packed with the merchandise (a fold-out carton is a display of this kind), (3) mailed to retailers, (4) distributed by wholesalers' and jobbers' salesmen, and (5) distributed by display crews, employed by the manufacturer or by a professional display-service organization.

Of the five methods listed, the first— distribution by manufacturers' salesmen—and the fifth— distribution by display crews—are the best. Most retailers are not trained in the art of dressing windows, arranging inside displays, or even hanging banners and flags, and so they welcome assistance.

If assistance in assembling point-of-purchase displays results in noticeable increases in sales or if a retailer believes that an increase was due to a display piece, then the manufacturer will receive preferred treatment with other displays that he distributes to the retailer, because the assistance can only be given by direct means of distribution.

The cost of providing professional display crews as a method of distributing point-of-purchase materials is quite high in comparison with that of the other methods. Whether the additional cost is worthwhile or not depends on the product, the market, and the retail situation. If the crews produce displays that are more effective, then they are worth the additional cost. If the manufacturer can do as well with one of the other methods of distribution, then he should not use the services of professional display crews.

Demonstrators

Retail demonstrations are an important means of attracting attention to a product. Nothing is better for most products than actually showing them in use.

Retail demonstrators are supplied by manufacturers. Some demonstrators are permanent but most go from store to store staying from two weeks to half a day at a particular store. They are usually hired and paid by manufacturers directly or supplied through an agency that specializes in supplying demonstrators.

There are two kinds of demonstrators. One is the kind who prepares and distributes the product (sometimes this is referred to as a retail sample). In this kind of demonstration an attempt is made to make consumers purchase a product, and the demonstrator attempts to make them try a sample. An example of this kind of demonstration is the giving away of brown 'n' serve sausages in a supermarket, or orange juice, or another product of this kind.

The other kind of demonstrator is the one who shows how a product works and attempts to make consumers purchase it. This kind of demonstrator normally shows prospective buyers how to use the product, how effectively it works, and the important points or merits that it has.

Although demonstrators act like salesmen, in that they give a pitch for a product, they are there to show it. The most important part of the demonstration as a sales promotion device is that customers must be convinced by seeing the product in use. Demonstrations of this kind are used particularly by manufacturers of cosmetics, appliances, and other products for which the decision to buy is affected by seeing them in use.

The cost of using demonstrations is quite high, like any form of sales promotion that uses direct labor, and so demonstrations are criticized as too costly. But the cost depends on how well demonstrations work for a manufacturer. If the demonstrations are successful, then they must be considered worth their cost; if not, then another method of sales promotion for these products must be found.

Demonstrations are important, and although they are not widely used, this does not mean that they are inefficient. Actually, for some kinds of products demonstrations are one of the most efficient means of promoting them at retail. Take, for example, the case of cosmetics in a department store or a large-volume drugstore. Here demonstrations are very important. Even modeling can be considered a form of demonstration, and it is widely used in the fashion industry.

Notes

1. Ralph S. Alexander and Thomas L. Berg, *Dynamic Management in Marketing*, Richard D. Irwin, Inc., Homewood, Ill., 1965, p. 57.

2. Richard Hammer, "Will Trading Stamps Stick?" *Fortune*, August, 1960, pp. 116ff.

3. "Trading Stamp Tumult," *Sales Management*, Dec. 1, 1966, p. 31.

4. Hammer, *op. cit.*, p. 116.

5. "Point-of-sale Material Increases Retailers' Sales," *Sales and Advertising Idea Library*, The National Research Bureau, Inc., September, 1962.

6. Charles J. Dirksen and Arthur Kroger, *Advertising Principles and Problems*, rev. ed., Richard D. Irwin, Inc., Homewood, Ill., 1964, pp. 516–517.

7. C. H. Sandage and Vernon Fryburger, *Advertising Theory and Practice*, 6th ed., Richard D. Irwin, Inc., Homewood, Ill., 1963, p. 498.

CHAPTER 6/PROMOTIONS TO THE TRADE

Trade deals are temporary sales promotion devices aimed at obtaining short-term merchandising advantages in retail stores or warehouses. In effect, trade deals encourage retailers to give a product additional selling support that it would not receive under normal retail selling and pricing conditions.

Among some manufacturers and retailers, trade deals are considered little less than bribery. Others, however, consider them a highly acceptable and productive merchandising incentive. Many manufacturers rightfully claim that a stimulus for retailers is built into the cost structure (margin) of merchandise. Some food items—for example, canned foods—may offer a 19 to 20 percent margin to retailers. Some drug items—for example, toothpaste—may offer a 30 to 40 percent margin. A few items—for example, certain pieces of furniture—may offer as high as a 75 or even 100 percent margin.

In these margins there is a recognition of the cost involved in the speed of product turnover, handling problems, shelf and floor space allocations, and retail selling and merchandising. Properly established, these margins adequately compensate retailers for their cooperation.

The fact that additional incentives are offered to retailers for certain merchandising services is a natural outgrowth of the competitiveness of the marketplace. Manufacturers want preferred store locations, special displays, and advertised features. New products and products with seasonal appeal especially benefit from such kinds of merchandising support. Because more manufacturers seek this kind of merchandising help than retailers can serve, the practice of trade dealing has grown in competitiveness.

The ethics of such trade deals is debatable, but their effectiveness is not. Like other sales promotion devices, trade deals can be misused and wasteful. However, they can also create additional sales and profit for both manufacturers and retailers.

There are certain advantages to the use of almost all the kinds of trade deals. First, they can be very effective in obtaining retail merchandising support. Directly in the form of money or indirectly, for example, in advertising and display allowances, they offer retailers an opportunity for increased profitability. Usually the greater the chance for more profit, the greater the degree of retailer cooperation.

A second advantage to trade deals is that they can be activated quickly. They do not involve time-consuming changes in packaging or preparation of media advertising or point-of-purchase materials. They merely require normal clearance with other departments in a corporation and an announcement to the sales force and trade.

Third, trade deals can focus on certain kinds of marketing problems that are beyond the capabilities of consumer promotions. For example, they can speed up or slow down inventories in order to influence consumer purchases rather than reflect them.

Fourth, and finally, trade deals can be combined with consumer promotions to stimulate retailer support. A merchandising allowance might be used with a price-off coupon promotion, for example.

The disadvantages of trade deals should also be noted. The most frequent deals are allowances of money or merchandise, and they are quite expensive. Moreover, cooperation does not always reach expected levels. Sometimes minimum support by wholesalers or retailers reduces their efficiency and increases the cost per unit sold. Also, when certain allowances are used to obtain temporary retail price reductions, the price reduction does not always follow. In such cases, retailers hold back all or part of the allowance rather than pass it along to consumers. Finally, trade deals are quite convenient and easy for marketing managers to use, and this encourages their use when other, more complicated promotion devices might better fulfill the objectives of a marketing plan.[1]

Deals or merchandise sales promotion devices

Deals are sales promotion devices aimed at obtaining retail distribution of a product. Their basic purpose is to stimulate retailers directly to carry the merchandise of a manufacturer. They are direct payments in either money or merchandise, and there are four basic kinds.

Buying allowance A buying allowance is a short-term and uncomplicated offer of a certain amount of money for a certain quantity of a product purchased. It is short-term because it aims at one or two larger-than-normal purchases by wholesalers or retailers. It is a temporary price reduction to them. That it is an uncomplicated offer means that no merchandising or advertising performance is requested of wholesalers or retailers. The purchase itself qualifies them for payment of the allowance. In simple terms, a buying allowance is an offer of 25 or 50 or more cents to wholesalers or retailers on each case, bale, or other quantity of product purchased during a stated period of time. Most important is that it is money, and this is its strength. It leads directly to a quickly realized, additional profit for wholesalers or retailers.

A buying allowance is often offered at the introduction of a new product. To call this buying distribution, as some marketers do, is to fail to recognize the intricacy of the marketing complex. To take on a new product, wholesalers or retailers in many lines of business must create a new slot in the warehouse and code it in a computer, and then they need a new card in the computer to record inventory levels. Shipping and ordering forms must be set up for retail outlets. Space must be provided on the selling floor or the store shelves. Especially in the tightly packed shelves of a food store, it may also be necessary to discontinue a slow-moving product to make room for a more promising newcomer. This again involves a series of changes in data processing and other administrative records. As a practical device, a buying allowance is a *sine qua non* for a new product, because wholesalers and retailers must have it to defray the initial expense of distributing a new product.

In addition to its use in obtaining distribution of a new product, a buying allowance can be used to achieve a quick and temporary drop in retail prices. Such a price drop may be needed to offset competitive merchandising activity, to protect shelf space against invasion by new products, to build tonnage or move excess inventory, or for other reasons. There is no guarantee that a buying allowance always brings about a lower retail price. Local competition among retailers is the deciding factor. The buying allowance may be kept in the treasury by wholesalers or retailers in relatively noncompetitive situations or passed on to consumers under highly volatile conditions. It is this uncertainty which gave rise to the price pack or cents-off deals which were previously described and which cannot be retained by retailers.

In evaluating the potential of a buying allowance as a sales promotion device for lowering retail prices or obtaining distribution of new products, one should not overlook its main objective. A buying allowance is meant to do what the term implies, encourage wholesalers or retailers to buy an item or a quantity of an item that they might not buy otherwise. In favor of a buying allowance is the fact that the money stays under the control of the buyer. He can use it for his own needs. For example, it can be turned to immediate profit, advertising, or a reduced price, as he wishes. This is not so with other kinds of sales promotion devices, in which the use of the money is dictated by the nature of the trade deal.

An advertising allowance is one of those trade deals in which the money involved is removed, at least ostensibly, from the control of the buyer and assigned to the advertising manager. It is the simplicity and directness of a buying allowance that appeals to wholesalers and retailers. In fact, attempts to tamper with this simplicity have met with mixed reactions. The most important involves escalated buying allowances— retailers may be offered 25 cents a case if they purchase one size of a brand, 50 cents a case on all sizes if they buy two sizes, and 75 cents or $1 a case on all sizes if they buy all three sizes.

Some retailers resist this kind of sales promotion device firmly and may refuse it entirely, either because it conflicts with their policy on sizes to be stocked or because they feel that it is unusual and unwarranted pressure from a supplier. Other retailers circumvent a buying allowance by buying minimal quantities of the larger sizes in order to qualify for the maximum allowance. Still other retailers cooperate with a supplier and accept and support a buying allowance enthusiastically. There is no doubt that as a complex sales promotion device an escalated buying allowance is more controversial than a simple one. However, it can still be quite effective particularly in encouraging multisized distribution in spite of predictable problems in trade relations.

There are two methods of paying wholesalers and retailers a buying allowance. A check may be issued, or the amount of the allowance may be deducted from the face of the invoice for the merchandise offered. The only difference in these two methods is that smaller retailers prefer a check, to help their cash flow, and wholesalers and larger retailers prefer the easier accounting of the second method.

Count and recount   A count and recount is an offer of a certain amount of money for each unit of merchandise moved out of a wholesaler's or retailer's warehouse in a specified period of time. For example, such a trade deal may consist of an allowance of 50 cents or $1 per case of vegetable shortening moved from a warehouse between April 1 and April 30. On a particular product, the money amount of the count and recount allowance is usually about the same as that offered on the same product as a buying or merchandise allowance— whatever the competitive situation requires. It is the cooperative action of retailers generated by the trade deal that changes, not the amount of money expended.

Because count and recount sales promotions are applied only to warehouse stocks, their objectives are rather narrow and specific. One aim of a count and recount is to flush warehouse inventory in order to forestall a possible out-of-stock situation on retail shelves. Often with new products that are unusually successful the sales at retail may exceed the speed of replacement, and a count and recount adds impetus to restocking. A count and recount can also be used to clear the distribution channels of an old product or package immediately before the introduction of an improved product or new package. Then again, there are times, particularly with less popular brands, when warehouse inventories become too large in relation to a product's turnover at retail. A count and recount can lower the warehouse inventory and reestablish a more efficient ratio of back-up stock to retail stock.

Here is a list of some of the advantages that a count and recount sales promotion offers, some of which are unique. First, payment is made only on a product moved and actually counted as moved. Second, a count and recount establishes a reduced inventory level against which a new order can be quickly activated. Also, a count and recount sometimes brings about a low retail price if retailers decide to use the money earned on this promotion to lower their prices, and thus helps empty retail shelves as well. One other advantage for manufacturers who initiate a count and recount is that no money is paid to wholesalers or retailers until the promotion is over. Payment is made only after verification of the recount.

Among the disadvantages, three are important. One is an inversion of the last-mentioned advantage for manufacturers. Retailers know that this sales promotion device is underwritten with their money and that they are paid only after the promotion is completed. A second disadvantage is that there is a possibility of faulty mathematics, either accidental or deliberately dishonest. Thus a manufacturer may pay for merchandise that is not actually moved out of a warehouse as agreed. A third disadvantage is that some retailers with small warehouses or those with such efficient warehouses that inventories are minimal may not be able to exploit this kind of device so well as those wholesalers or retailers which are not so large or efficient.

The producers in a count and recount sales promotion require two calls by their salesmen, who take an initial and a closing count of merchandise in inventory. Before records of inventories were maintained by computers, salesmen made a count and recount of actual cases of a product in warehouses. More modern systems now permit the inspection of cards from a computer or other office records at the time of the count and again at the recount. Payment for the merchandise moved, based on the difference between the count and recount figures, is almost always made by check.

Buy-back allowance A buy-back allowance immediately follows another trade deal and offers a certain amount of money for new purchases based on the quantity of purchases made on the first trade deal. The buy-back is a satellite trade promotion which encourages repurchase of a product immediately after another trade deal. The buy-back is a tail appended to another sales promotion. For example, a coffee manufacturer might announce a sales promotion trade deal that combines a count and recount and a buy-back allowance. The count and recount might be in an amount of $1 a case moved from April 1 to April 30. The buy-back might also be for $1 a case, or another appropriate amount, for the first one or two orders placed after April 30 and not later than May 15. The quantity of merchandise purchased on the buy-back may not exceed that moved on the count and recount. This last stipulation ties the promotions together and uses the second to stimulate more product movement from the first.

In looking for the proper use of a buy-back, one should remember its objectives. First, it greatly strengthens a buyer's motivation to cooperate on the first trade deal, because he will qualify for a greater buy-back. Second, assuming that the first trade deal sells some of a product through retailers, a buy-back restocks inventories.

Because a buy-back is a resale opportunity, it extends the life of a trade deal and helps prevent a postdeal sales decline. It also ensures aggressive implementation of both promotions by the sales force, which is committed to soliciting buy-back orders and hence to following the progress of the trade deal.

One negative consideration is the expense. A buy-back adds one allowance to another. Each allowance must offer an amount of money as large or almost as large as in an independent trade deal, or the promotion loses competitiveness. A second negative consideration is that a buy-back may reestablish a postdeal sales decline if the allowances are advantageous to the buyer. This is particularly likely when a buy-back is combined with a count and recount. A third negative consideration is in the timing of the announcement of the trade deal. A buy-back is necessarily announced at the same time as the first sales promotion so that the two can work together. The early announcement provides a great deal of time for competitors to plan and inaugurate countermoves to blunt the buy-back.

Like a buying allowance, a buy-back is paid to wholesalers or retailers by check or by reduction from the face of the invoice. However, its effectiveness can be shortened or lengthened by changing the terms of the sale. A buy-back as a trade deal can be applied to any orders in a 15- or 30-day period. The decision to shorten or lengthen its impact arises from the inventory needs of the promoter.

In practice, buy-back sales promotion devices are not used very often. They obviously budget the cost of two promotions in one promotion time period, but because of their unusual nature and concentrated power, they can, in fact, dominate the sales promotion scene for the period of the trade deal's life.

Free goods   A free-goods trade deal is an offer of a certain amount of a product to wholesalers or retailers at no cost to them but dependent on the purchase of a stated amount of the same or another product. Simply, goods or a product is given to wholesalers or retailers instead of money. In fact, free goods can be substituted for money in almost any allowance. Like money allowances, free-goods deals vary in strength and frequency depending on their cost and the competition. Baker's dozen, 1 free with 11, 2 free with 10, are common free-goods deals. Less common but still noteworthy are 1 free with 3 or 1 for 1.

Free goods are really another form of payment of a sales promotion. They can be used on a buying allowance, count and recount, merchandising allowance, and the like. As a kind of payment they are mathematically attractive. Although retailers can sell them at full price, the manufacturer's contribution is only the cost of the merchandise. Free goods, however, are not quite so attractive as money in trade-deal payments, because there are some handling costs and bookkeeping complications. In order to avoid these negative factors and implement free goods as simply as possible, the deal is usually made through the invoice. Wholesalers or retailers pay only for the merchandise that they purchase. Then shipment to warehouses includes both the purchased merchandise and the free goods.

Advertising and display allowances

Advertising and display allowances are those trade deals which are used to induce wholesalers and retailers to promote a product through advertising and display. Basically, there are only three kinds.

Merchandise allowances A merchandise allowance is a short-term, contractual agreement through which a manufacturer compensates wholesalers or retailers for advertising or in-store display of his products.[2] The advertising or displays are known as features. A merchandising allowance aims at obtaining them in one of three ways.

First, there is an advertising allowance in which distributors give a manufacturer some kind of advertising support in return for a merchandise allowance. The support may be an inclusion of the manufacturer's product in their newspaper ads, radio programs, handbills, or other vehicles. Second, there is a display allowance in which retailers qualify for payment from a manufacturer by building special displays for his product. Third, and most common, a merchandise allowance is offered to retailers for featuring a manufacturer's product in their advertising or displays. For manufacturers, these features can produce a very modest (10 percent)[3] or a very large sales increase (over 40 percent). For retailers, the range of profitability is also wide. In fact, they can lose money or realize a handsome profit, depending on margins, handling costs, and the like.

The promise of greatly increased volume is enough to spur manufacturers on in their pursuit of features, which may mean more sales to present customers and trial by new customers as a result of advertising or convenient display locations in stores. However, the true lure of features is the opportunity for immense volume increases.

Not all products are likely candidates for merchandise allowances. Some low-volume or specialty items may sell almost as well off the shelf as off a display or from an ad. Other items are too bulky to earn a good profit on the valuable space occupied. Frozen and refrigerated products, although often advertised, are seldom sold from separate displays because of the awkwardness and expense of freezer cases.

Although it is the manufacturer who devises sales promotions aimed at features and displays, it is retailers who must select a few promotions for support among a great number (often over 100) offered them each week. In their selection for merchandising support, retailers must weigh a set of complex factors. High-volume products are desirable. High-profit items are, too. Products that are easy to handle are better than those which are not. The special price, if any, is another factor. Most often, no single candidate rates highly on all counts. Hence, although there are guidelines and even formulas of a sort developed to sharpen decisions, the judgment of retailers is the final determinant.

The disadvantages for a manufacturer who sponsors merchandise allowances are very real. Merchandising support on the part of retailers is often minimal. Newspaper features may be little one- or two-line notices. These half-hearted features are sometimes derisively called *obituary ads*. Then, too, display features are sometimes actually erected in a relatively small percentage of the stores in a chain or voluntary group. A manufacturer thus pays an allowance on all cases sold and receives only partial support. Another disadvantage is that retailers buy their advertising at special low rates but bill a manufacturer at the high rates that apply to national advertisers. There may be a 30 to 40 percent difference between retail and national rates. This differential was and is a matter of some irritation to manufacturers but has become an accepted practice.

One will always hear the words "proof of performance" in connection with merchandise allowances. This proof is the essence of advertising and display promotions in that retailers are asked not only to perform a service for the money but also to certify it before payment. In advertising allowances, retailers usually furnish a tear sheet of their advertisement showing the manufacturer's product or a radio or television affidavit of broadcasting with the invoice. On display features, retailers furnish written certification of compliance with the terms of the agreement. Performance may not always be maximal but it always involves some retail effort and is sometimes quite effective.

Cooperative advertising   Cooperative advertising is characterized by a long-term contract in which a manufacturer agrees to pay an allowance to retailers for each case or other unit of product purchased during the life of the contract. Retailers agree to run advertisements periodically in the amount of the allowances due them. In practice, retailers are not paid until the ads are run and they submit proof or affidavits of performance with the invoice from the media in which the ads were run. Until the proof and invoices are submitted retailers' accumulations of cooperative allowances are, in effect, held by the sponsor of the promotion.[4]

The confines of cooperative advertising are much narrower than those of a merchandising allowance. A contract may last a year or more, and it is usually restricted to advertising and does not cover other forms of promotion, including displays. Cooperative advertising is not aimed at a short-term, display advantage. However, some contracts are more restrictive in their interpretation of the word "advertising" than others. Newspaper and radio and television advertising is specified in some contracts, but others are looser and include handbills, shoppers' papers, and point-of-purchase materials as acceptable advertising media. Generally, these less orthodox advertising vehicles are permitted for the benefit of retailers who are too small or so located that the more commonly used media are uneconomical or restricted.

Although retailers use cooperative-advertising allowances to increase the funds available to them for advertising and promotion, the manufacturer also aims for regular retail advertising features. One may argue about the principle involved, that manufacturers should not, in effect, pay retailers' advertising bills. However, the practice exists to such a great extent that its competitiveness will surely sustain cooperative advertising. Hence, a more rewarding approach to the problem would be to concentrate on making cooperative advertising more effective. Let us, then, look at some of the problems involved and also consider some good practices that have been instituted by manufacturers in an attempt to remedy the situation.

Among these problems none is more serious than the practice of retailers of jamming a great number of features into an ad. In some recent checks of food ads in Chicago newspapers, 83 features were counted in a double-truck ad, and the single-page ads contained an average of 42 features or obituary ads. It is almost inconceivable that these small ads do anything more than permit retailers to fulfill their agreement minimally in order to collect the accumulated cooperative-advertising funds.

So many cooperative-advertising contracts are in the market that the task of cramming a host of four- or five-line notices into a weekly ad is overwhelming for retail ad managers. In these instances, the eagerly sought additional support of retailers becomes meaningless and ineffective for both manufacturers and retailers. Only retailers gain from this overcrowding of ads, and their gain is based on the practice of making money by buying space at local rates and billing the sponsor at national rates.

The spread in the rate between retail and national advertising may be enough to cover all retailer ad costs, perhaps with a small profit for retailers as well. But the practice of having two rate structures is currently under attack and may be tested in the courts shortly to determine if it is not illegal under the antitrust laws.

Among the problems that also face the manufacturer who uses cooperative advertising is that it can deplete the regular advertising budget. The money spent on a mention of a product and its price in a dull and visually confusing retail newspaper ad is diverted from more expertly prepared national advertising. Then, too, the administration of cooperative advertising is costly and occasionally a source of disagreement and friction between a manufacturer and retailers.

Although many of the problems in cooperative advertising cannot be resolved without a complete reconstruction of the program as we know it, many steps can be taken to reduce the influence of the negative factors and, to a large extent, increase the effectiveness of the program. For example, when retailers run a cooperative ad, they should use it as one element in a total promotion. Price promotions, premiums, and other offers can be added to give meaning and merchantability to the ad. Another improvement has been instituted by manufacturers to provide better budget planning for retailers. Funds are not required to be used on a current basis but are accumulated in one calendar quarter against use in the following quarter. More farsighted planning is thus encouraged.

In the same vein, the planning of retailers also benefits from good advance announcement of a promotion—four to six weeks is minimal. There is every opportunity to obtain a major feature—an important ad within the retailer's ad—rather than an "obituary" ad if promising promotions are presented to the trade well in advance of their scheduled dates and if the method of accumulating money has permitted the establishment of an available kitty.

Dealer-listing promotions   Dealer-listing promotions are unique among the two general classes of trade deals concerning advertising that we have described, because they are directed almost equally at retailers and consumers. The influence of dealer-listing promotions on retailers can usually be measured precisely, and because of their ability to activate retailers quickly, we classify them as trade promotions. However, their consumer influence is not considerably less.

A dealer-listing promotion is an advertisement that carries a selling message on a product or a consumer promotion and also announces the names and sometimes the addresses of retailers who stock the product or who are cooperating in the promotion. Advertisements of this kind with many, even hundreds, of names of participating retailers often appear in newspapers and magazines. On radio and television ads only a smaller number of retailers can be listed because of the limited time available in each announcement. In all cases the purpose of the dealer-listing promotions is dual. They aim at announcing a product innovation or promotion to consumers and also inform the same consumers where the product can be purchased or the promotion sought. Also, they aim at convincing retailers that they should stock the product or cooperate in the promotion precisely because prospective consumers will see the list of dealers and select one to visit to buy the product or participate in the promotion. This is, then, a traffic-building promotion for retailers.

There is no payment of money or goods to retailers in this kind of promotion. They are compensated only through the publishing of their name and address in the advertising medium used in the sales promotion. In fact, in some cases, retailers are willing to contribute some of their own money or cooperative advertising funds to pay for the listings.

Clearly, this kind of promotion is useful in the introduction of new products and the exploitation of consumer promotions. The Parker Pen Company, for example, used dealer listings to introduce the highly successful Parker T-Ball Jotter. In this instance, the listing of drugstores, stationery stores, and department stores built distribution for the product and stimulated consumer purchases. The mechanics of this promotion included a mailing piece to retailers soliciting an order for several dozen pens and promising a dealer listing in an ad in return for the order. Retailers who did not respond to the mail solicitation were then visited by a sales crew. Overall, product distribution in these outlets rose from 42 percent to 78 percent in a four-week promotion period.

Dealer-listing promotions are difficult to administer, and, particularly, they consume a large amount of sales-force time in setting them up. However, if a manufacturer is able to accept these burdens, dealer listings are a good sales promotion device and can deliver good results in a short time.

Direct stimulants of retailers and retail salesmen

This sales promotion device is used to stimulate retailers and their salesmen to push a manufacturer's product rather than that of a competitor. There are three kinds: one is money or merchandise to pay salesmen for their effort; another is a contest where the prizes are valuable and are obtained by selling a certain quantity of a manufacturer's goods; and finally there is a tie-in of merchandise for dealers for pushing or promoting a manufacturer's product.

PMs or push money   A PM (premium money, sometimes called a *spiff*) is a special incentive to salesmen to push a line of goods. It is given in addition to normal compensation as a reward for selling.

For example, if an appliance manufacturer wishes to have his line of washing machines pushed at retail, he may offer a PM of $10 per unit to salesmen. The PM is an incentive for them to sell his washing machines instead of a competitor's.

There are some problems in the use of PMs. Many retailers do not like push money, because they feel that salesmen may sell a line of goods rather than their whole line of merchandise. They also feel that the practice of PMs leads to unbalanced stock and salesmen looking only for their allowance.

From a manufacturer's viewpoint a PM is an added cost. It is not only paid on additional sales but also on all sales whether salesmen push the line or not. There is no doubt that in some cases it is an unnecessary expense.

The greatest value of a PM is that it reaches the most important point in the channel of distribution, the key person in the selling mechanism for goods that depend on the sales person. Nothing is stronger than salesmen being on a manufacturer's side.

Naturally this form of incentive cannot be used effectively with self-service goods or goods of low value. With these goods salesmen do not have any influence on purchases, and other forms of promotion should be used.

Sales contests   A sales promotion device that is used to stimulate and motivate distributors, retailers, and their salesmen is the sales contest. The sales contest has wide appeal and has been used successfully in many businesses. The most important aspect of the sales contest is that it represents recognition and reward for outstanding accomplishment.[5]

To make a channel-of-distribution sales contest work effectively, there must be a chance of winning for all who are eligible to enter. The contest cannot be a lottery but must be based solely on the amount of goods sold by each participant. By making the goal of the contest a percentage of increase or amount over quota by ratio rather than the total amount sold, a manufacturer allows even young or junior salesmen or small retailers to have a chance at the prize. Many contests now being offered have substantial prizes, such as Lincoln Continentals and trips to Europe. These are not single prizes but a group of similar prizes in which many contestants can win.

The value of the sales contest is that, if all the members or units in the channel of distribution participate in it and sales increase only a minimum amount in each unit, then the amount of sales dollar increases will pay for the contest prizes easily. The real success of the sales contest is to get as many participants as possible. A large number of participants is needed to give a manufacturer his expected boost.

There are also problems in sales contests, as in all forms of sales promotion. Although it motivates salesmen, retailers, or wholesalers, the sales contest is economically unsound; that is, the manufacturer in a sales contest pays for a job that he has already paid for.

Another criticism of the sales contest is that it is merely a temporary shot in the arm for distribution and has little if any long-term value. It would be necessary to have many sales contests, again and again, to have a lasting effect.

One of the troublesome things about sales contests is that manufacturers consider them easy. Many promotion managers feel that all that is necessary to make a contest successful is to make the offer. But contests, like all marketing and sales promotion activities, need to be properly planned and executed. Some of the important considerations are: [6]

1. Determine the contest objectives
2. Decide on the length of the contest
3. Select who should participate in the contest
4. Choose the prizes
5. Pick the theme
6. Promote the contest

7. Run the contest
8. Pay off promptly
9. Evaluate the contest results

Dealer loaders   A dealer loader is a premium that is presented to retailers for the purchase of certain quantities of merchandise. There are two kinds: (1) Buying loaders, which are gifts given in return for an order. This is unabashed, out-and-out wheeling and dealing. In value, these loaders have ranged from a doll worth $3 to an automobile worth $3,000. (2) Display loaders, which are an integral part of a display and, secondarily, a gift for retailers or store managers.

The purpose of a buying loader is to gain new distribution or to sell an unusually large quantity of goods. A manufacturer may anticipate a heavy seasonal demand for his product, or, in fact, he may be a victim of his own overproduction. For these and other reasons he may wish to sell an unusually large amount of merchandise in a short time and may turn to a buying loader as a more economical sales promotion device than a buying allowance. The money-saving factor is that the manufacturer may buy the loader premiums in quantity and at an advantageous price. The premium is viewed at its retail value by the recipient, and the sponsor may have benefited up to 40 or 50 percent in cost savings.[7]

A display loader, as indicated, is part of a special display. By offering the premium as a part of an attractive display piece, a manufacturer hopes to obtain a special display and move an additional amount of merchandise. After the display has been dismantled, the premium is given to the store manager, department manager, or the owner as a bonus. In 1965 the Minnesota Valley Canning Company offered a stuffed-doll version of the Jolly Green Giant as a display loader. In some instances, it is worth noting that the premium displayed may also be offered as a self-liquidating premium to consumers. The premium and the display thus serve each other. The premium helps the display, and the display is a visual selling aid for the self-liquidating premium.

The chief limitation of display loaders in the food field is that they can usually be implemented only through independently owned stores or in chains with a few stores. The large chains prefer deals that can be controlled at, and are of benefit to, the operating headquarters. Not only do display loaders deprive the headquarters of potential revenue, but they also diminish the headquarter's control of merchandise and display planning for their retail outlets. With other kinds of retailers—lawn and garden supply dealers, department stores, and the like—this limitation is not so severe. A second negative factor is the implication of bribery, particularly if the premiums encourage personal advantage rather than utility in the business involved.

Notes

1. Paul D. Converse, Harvey W. Huegy, and Robert V. Mitchell, *Elements of Marketing,* 6th ed., Prentice-Hall, Inc., Englewood Cliffs, N.J., 1958, p. 604.

2. "FTC Okays Plan to Reimburse for Store Ads on Traffic Basis," *Advertising Age,* Sept. 26, 1966, p. 54.

3. "The Dillon Study," *Progressive Grocer,* 1960, pp. 4–7.

4. Otto Kleppner, *Advertising Procedure,* 5th ed., Prentice-Hall, Inc., Englewood Cliffs, N.J., 1966, pp. 427–430.

5. "Incentives: Selling's Mighty Motivators," *Sales Management,* Sept. 10, 1966, p. 90.

6. "Modern Management and the Urge to Succeed," *Sales Management,* Dec. 10, 1966, pp. 25–27.

7. "Dealer Loaders, Prizes, Gifts Spur Selling," *Advertising Age,* Dec. 12, 1966, p. 39.

CHAPTER 7/LEGAL ASPECTS OF SALES PROMOTION AND MERCHANDISING

This chapter is a short explanation in layman's terms of the more frequently encountered legal aspects of sales promotions. The material given here is not intended as a substitute for an attorney's advice but as encouragement to seek a lawyer's opinion on legal matters dealing with the use of sales promotion and merchandising devices. The laws governing the use of sales promotions are destined for many changes in a consumer-oriented economy, and the interrelationship of these laws, if they follow the practice of previous legislation affecting marketing, may become fine in point, complex in development, and, at times, unfortunately ambiguous.

If this chapter serves only one useful purpose well, it should discourage the legal dilettante and encourage the solicitation of qualified legal opinion. It would be impossible for any book to give legal advice on a subject as diversified as sales promotion, and so all that is attempted here is to give a summary of the background and major legislation and interpretation of certain laws as they pertain to the use of sales promotions.

Legal background of laws pertaining to sales promotion and merchandising

Before examining the laws and regulations pertaining to sales promotion and merchandising, a brief review of the historical and economic justification for the antitrust acts is necessary. For a free, competitive system to survive in the late 1800s and early 1900s curbs were needed on the freedom of enterprise because of abuses of competition or the lack of it.

For the encouragement of economic growth, giant industry needed to be regulated to get fair and equitable treatment for all industry. The concept of economic growth in the

1800s in the United States was *laissez-faire*. Literally interpreted at that time laissez-faire meant let nothing stand in the way of business growth. Anything was good for economic growth that showed economic utility and produced business growth and progress.

Under the philosophy of laissez-faire some manufacturers did, in fact, restrain trade and seriously inhibit competition. Some manufacturers did, in fact, engage in deceptive business practices. Laws were thus needed in each case of deceptive practice to avoid monopolism and to protect the rights of the individual.

The basic law governing restraint of trade and monopoly in interstate and foreign commerce is the Sherman Antitrust Act of 1890, which legally acknowledges that completely free competition defeats itself when it evolves into monopolism. Nothing can better express this idea than the first section of the Sherman Act:

> Every contract, combination in the form of trust or otherwise, or conspiracy, in restraint of trade or commerce among the several States, or with foreign nations, is hereby declared to be illegal. Every person who shall make such contract or engage in any such combination or conspiracy shall be deemed guilty of a misdemeanor, and, on conviction thereof, shall be punished by fine not exceeding fifty thousand dollars, or by imprisonment not exceeding one year, or by both said punishments, in the discretion of the court.

In 1914, another act of Congress was passed to encourage competition in business. This was the Federal Trade Commission Act, which established the Federal Trade Commission as an investigative and prosecuting agency and gave it the power to enforce the laws under its jurisdiction—the Federal Trade Commission Act, the Clayton Act, the Webb-Pomerene Export Act, the Flammable Fabrics Act, and the wool, fur, and textile-fiber products labeling acts.

The Commission utilizes administrative regulations to establish rules of conduct for business practice. These administrative regulations are usually handed down as guides or procedures. If they are not followed, the Commission can issue cease-and-desist orders. The areas in which the Commission administrates are restraints of trade and deceptive business practices.

The Clayton Act, also passed by Congress in 1914, is an important extension of the Sherman Antitrust Act. The Clayton Act prohibits price discrimination, tying and exclusive agreements, and the acquisition of the stock of another corporation when these activities might tend to reduce competition or encourage monopolism. By intent and wording, the Clayton Act had a more limiting effect on business than previous laws. However, it was soon apparent that an even more comprehensive delineation was needed.

In the early 1930s, the depression years, some chain grocery stores were able to negotiate special price advantages on the basis of their volume purchasing. They offered lower retail prices and, especially, in a depression economy, attracted enough volume from consumers to endanger the survival of smaller, independent grocers. This practice, as followed by distributors to chains, was considered by independent grocers to be unfair because it was based on price discrimination. The special price advantage that chain stores could command from manufacturers tended to reduce competition for independent grocers. It was argued that the practice of price discrimination for chains encouraged monopolism and restraint of trade against independent grocers. Congress, responsive to public opinion, enacted a new law in 1936 to curb the advantage of chain stores.

This was the Robinson-Patman Act. It was passed as an amendment to Section 2 of the Clayton Act, which deals with price discrimination. Congressional action, in passing the Robinson-Patman Act, was precipitated by extreme aggressiveness on the part of certain retailers. However, because sellers solicit retailers and publish their agreements and terms of sale, the Robinson-Patman Act imposed its restrictions on sellers rather than buyers. The act is more enforceable in this way, and violations are more traceable. In fact, the Robinson-Patman Act does prohibit a buyer from knowingly accepting a discrimination in price, but its main purpose is to control price discrimination at the level of the seller.

A clear rationale for the new legislation is expressed by

Earl W. Kintner [1] in *An Antitrust Primer:* "The Robinson-Patman Act is sometimes praised, sometimes abused, much interpreted, little understood, and capable of producing instant arguments of infinite variety. In many business quarters, the very name is an anathema." There can be little doubt that the Robinson-Patman Act is both complicated and controversial. Two justices of the Supreme Court of the United States recently made statements dealing with its ambiguity. Justice Frankfurter once said of it that, "Precision of expression is not an outstanding characteristic of this Act." Many agree.

Nevertheless, a clear interpretation of the Robinson-Patman Act is necessary in view of the complexities of the business world. If the Robinson-Patman Act had not been passed, it would be necessary to invent one now or something close to it. Therefore, however much we may decry the law's effect, it must be recognized that necessity justifies its primary objectives:

1. To prevent unscrupulous suppliers from attempting to gain an unfair advantage over their competitors by discriminating among buyers

2. To prevent unscrupulous buyers from using their economic power to exact discriminatory prices from suppliers to the disadvantage of less powerful buyers

Direct application of legal restraints to sales promotion and merchandising

The legislation that directly affects sales promotion and merchandising practices can be applied to devices that are used to motivate consumers as well as those which affect the trade. Certain legislative acts affect the use of sales promotion devices as these laws allow or restrict the practice with consumers. For example, a contest or sweepstakes is legal, but a lottery is illegal as a sales promotion device under Federal statute as well as most state statutes.

There is also legislation that affects the trade, particularly that which affects manufacturers who sell to wholesalers and retailers. Most of the later antitrust acts are concerned with the legal aspects of selling and buying so far as sales promotion devices give an advantage to one buyer that is not given to others.

Laws which affect the channel of distribution for sales promotion and merchandising practices The Sherman Act and the Clayton Act both prohibit discrimination in pricing that tends to or actually forms a monopoly or a restraint in trade. Neither act, however, holds that advertising, promotion, or merchandise allowances, payments, or services are, in effect or in part, price or affect price. But the Robinson-Patman Act, in Sections 2(d) and 2(e), covers the fact that by discrimination in allowances, payments, or services sellers may actually create or tend to create a monopoly or a restraint in trade:

> (d) That it shall be unlawful for any person engaged in commerce to pay or contract for the payment of anything of value to or for the benefit of a customer of such person in the course of such commerce as compensation or in consideration for any services or facilities furnished by or through such customer in connection with the processing, handling, sale, or offering for sale of any products or commodities manufactured, sold, or offered for sale by such person, unless such payment or consideration is available on proportionally equal terms to all other customers competing in the distribution of such products or commodities.
>
> (e) That it shall be unlawful for any person to discriminate in favor of one purchaser against another purchaser or purchasers of a commodity bought for resale, with or without processing, by contracting to furnish or furnishing, or by contributing to the furnishings of, any services of facilities connected with the processing, handling, sale, or offering for sale of such commodity so purchased upon terms not accorded to all purchasers on proportionally equal terms.

For all intents and purposes Sections 2(d) and 2(e) of the Robinson-Patman Act provide that, if a seller offers advertising, promotion, or merchandise allowances, payments, or services to one customer, he must offer them to all his customers on proportionally equal terms. Further, the offer has to be made to all competing customers, that is, those wholesalers or retailers who would tend to sell to the same buyers, and these allowances, payments, or services must be of equal quality as well as quantity.

To comply with the law, it is necessary to meet the three provisions of Sections 2(d) and 2(e) of the Robinson-Patman Act. But what is the meaning of each? First, what is meant by the phrase that the offer must be made available? It has been held that, to comply with the law, sellers must make an effort to inform all their customers of an offer, and this effort must be reasonable, so that all their customers know that the offer has been made available to them.

For example, if a buying allowance is offered to the large chains, it must also be offered to all other customers. But the method of notification may become part of the intention of the offer. If the seller notifies the chains by a letter that is sent by first-class mail and all other customers by stuffing a notification of the offer into their next shipment of merchandise, then it might be construed that the offer was not made available on an equal basis. The method of communication was not the same, and it might result in only the chains' knowing about the offer. This practice might be considered unfair.

Second, the advertising, promotion, or merchandise allowances, payments, or services must be made to all customers who compete with one another. Competition and the coverage of those who are competing with one another are a main point of this part of the law. Coverage must be tested in two ways. The first part of the test is whether buyers actually compete for the same customers. A seller is required to offer advertising, promotion, or merchandise allowances, payments, or services to all competing buyers if the offer is made to one of them. Competing buyers are those who will sell the goods that are purchased or those which are facilitated by a purchase to the same clientele.

The second part of the test is whether the offer can be used by all buyers or whether it is so designed that only one can take advantage of it. If the offer can be used by only one buyer or a small group of buyers and is not practical for others, then it might not be allowed under the law. The rule of practicality is that the offer can be used by a majority of buyers or that the manufacturer or seller must offer an alternative to those buyers who cannot use the primary plan or program.

The application of the availability of a sales promotion device must be examined in the light of the two parts of the test of coverage. An example of the first part would be whether buyers actually have the same customers and, if they do, whether their customers compete for the same products. This might be judged by the geographical location of buyers or by the clientele of wholesalers. A department store in Boston does not compete with one in Chicago, but one on the Avenue of the Americas in New York does compete with one on Third Avenue in the same city. But a wholesaler in Boston may have the same clientele for the same products in New York State as does a Chicago wholesaler. In this case, the two wholesalers compete with each other.

As for the second part of the test of coverage, if it were obvious that the offer was tailored for some buyers but not others, then it would not pass. For example, if it was available only to buyers who did a total business of $50,000 per month and had at least 12 outlets in specific geographical locations and only one buyer qualified under these terms, then the test of practicability would not be met.

Another example would be an advertising allowance offered to all buyers on the basis of how much each bought and all participated. But this offer could not be used by small retailers, because the amount of merchandise that they bought would not allow them enough money to use the allowance effectively. Such an advertising allowance might be perfectly legal if a number of buyers could participate. If, however, only one or a few of the buyers could take advantage of it, then it might not be allowed.

The third part of Sections 2(e) and 2(f) of the Robinson-Patman Act deals with the requirements that all advertising, promotion, or merchandise allowances, payments, or services must be made available to competing customers on "proportionally equal terms." [2] But what is the concept of proportional but equal? The act does not state what the proportion must be equal to or what the payments, allowances, or services must be equal to. The Federal Trade Commission's *Guide on Advertising and Promotional Allowances* states that generally the requirement on proportional but equal can best be met by basing the payments made, allowances offered, or services furnished on the dollar volume or the quantity of goods purchased over a period of time.

There is another problem in this concept of proportional but equal in that, in offering different kinds of sales promotion devices to different classes of retailers, is the seller being proportional but equal? Let us look at the problem in offering a demonstrator to a department store. In maintaining a demonstrator in, for example, the cosmetics department of a department store doing a volume business, what is the proportional but equal sales promotion device for a small-volume drugstore? If it is to be proportional in time, it might be five minutes a week of the demonstrator's time. So the manufacturer gives a money payment for display in proportion to the cost of the demonstrator's time for the department store according to the amount of purchase of both buyers. Is this equal? The equality of this situation depends on who looks at the allowance and how much it is.

In some cases the department store will say that this situation is not equal, because it would rather have a money payment instead of the demonstrator. Now where is the manufacturer? The lack of a definition of the proportional but equal concept creates a problem of how to use these sales promotion devices effectively and still stay within the law.

The manufacturer offering advertising, promotion, or merchandise allowances, payments, or services has the additional problem of making sure that every customer participating in such a program uses the benefits that he receives for the intended purpose. This means that the manufacturer has to police the buyer when an offer is given to be sure that it is not taken by the buyer as a price discount. For if the manufacturer does not control the offer, he and the buyer might be equally guilty of discrimination in price.

Now it should be obvious that the enforcement of the use of the offer is difficult. First, there is the problem of the relationship of the seller to the buyer in which the seller does not wish to alienate the buyer, particularly in a competitive situation. Yet according to the law and the interpretation of the Federal Trade Commission, the seller must enforce the proper use of the offer although the enforcement may cause him to lose customers.

A second consideration comes into the relationship of the seller to the buyer in handling the offer. Determining whether the buyer has used it properly is sometimes difficult. When the retailer uses a major medium, the manufacturer usually wants a bill from the medium and either a tear sheet of the ad or a verification that the ad has actually run. Unfortunately, some media give two bills, one for actual payment by the retailer and another, at a higher rate, to be given to the manufacturer. Verifications of the ads have also been falsified. If something other than a major medium is used, such as in-store displays, banners, or balloons, then the manufacturer has to take the word of the retailer that the allowances or payments have been used for the purpose for which they were intended.

The interpretation and administration of the legislation dealing with the proper use of offers has caused problems for manufacturers using them. The problems have not eliminated or even curtailed the use of sales promotion devices, but manufacturers have been using them rather cautiously and they sometimes look for the sales promotion device that will be least offensive to the Federal Trade Commission.

The purpose of the Robinson-Patman Act or the other legislation affecting sales promotions or the interpretation of the courts of this legislation was not to curtail their use or force manufacturers to use certain kinds of sales promotion devices. Its purpose was to eliminate monopoly or restraint of trade. But the circumvention of the regulatory bodies has become the practice in the trade, and this is how manufacturers and retailers play the game.

Legal aspects which affect consumer sales promotion devices
There are other legal aspects that affect consumer sales promotion devices. Unfortunately, there are some very deceptive practices that occasionally appear in one form or another in

their use. These deceptive practices are either illegal or tend to be very close to unethical practice.

Although some legal aspects of contests and sweepstakes have already been discussed, all were not covered. What was not covered are some of the deceptions sometimes found there. A contest or a sweepstakes is a perfectly legal and an acceptable means of sales promotion. The problem comes up when the contest turns into a lottery. A lottery is illegal under most state laws and also under Section 5 of the Federal Trade Commission Act.

The difference between a lottery and a contest is that in a lottery there must be a consideration, there must be a distribution of prizes, and the awards and prizes must be made by lot or chance.[3] In a contest or sweepstakes as used in sales promotion there should not be any consideration, that is, payment made to participate. One of the emphasized points in the gasoline giveaways or sweepstakes is that there is no purchase required in order to participate and that the only requirement is usually that only licensed automobile drivers are eligible. In most contests or sweepstakes as used in sales promotion, the consideration is normally waived, but the other two elements of a lottery are still present. However, because of the absence of consideration the contest or sweepstakes cannot now be considered a lottery, and therefore it is legal under the laws that forbid lotteries in most states. In a recent opinion in Ohio, the attorney-general held that "schemes of chance" and "cash give-aways" are illegal, because they violate the state's antigambling laws.[4]

The major problem in contests and sweepstakes as sales promotion devices is that there tends to be deception in their use that is unfair to consumers. These deceptions are (1) overstating the value of the merchandise offered as prizes, (2) misstating the rules and requirements or presenting them in opaque language, (3) overstating the opportunities for winning or the odds of winning so that consumers are not aware of the probability of success.

Any of the three deceptions may make the contest illegal under either Federal or state statute according to the infraction or the legislation being considered. But more important than the actual unlawfulness of the deceptions is that the Federal Trade Commission comes into the picture and sets standards for conduct.[5] A guide for the use of contests and sweepstakes is forthcoming.

Price-off promotions, too, have been used deceptively. Price-off promotions are particularly noted in the area of bait advertising and comparative pricing. In the use of price-off promotions the price must be really different for the sales and not simply a device to attract consumers to the product.[6] The Federal Trade Commission views price-off promotions in the same light as it does bait advertising if the price-off tends to be deceptive. The Commission has also issued a guide covering the price-off factors and when they can be used without being deceptive. Also many of the states have laws that affect the deceptive use of price-off sales promotions.

A third abuse of sales promotion has appeared with the introduction of certain new products in the packaged goods field. This abuse has occurred with two kinds of consumer sales promotions—cents-off and free samples offered on new product introductions. For example, a new product may be introduced in food stores or drugstores and labeled "7 cents off regular price." Similarly, a new product may be packaged three in a box or sleeve and labeled "One free with two. You save 30 cents." Such sales promotion devices are not deceptive on established products but are surely so on new products because in the introductory stage there is no recognized or known retail price for them. The preferred discount or bonus purchase has no meaning or value to consumers who are unaware of the basic value of the item. Legal advice might suggest that 60 days or 90 days after introduction this kind of sales promotion would be acceptable, but it is unlikely that clearance could be obtained any earlier in a new product introduction.

A fourth abuse of the sales promotion program is the combination offer. In this kind of offer the customer expects to receive two products for the price of one or an additional product for an added cost that is below the cost of the additional product. If the combination offer is that the additional product is without cost to the customer, then the price of the combination offer must be equal to the price of the primary item, that is, the total price of the primary product.

If the combination offer is that the price is increased to cover the cost of the secondary item, the price must be the value of the two items together; that is, the price cannot exceed the price of the two items sold separately, or the price must be equal to the value of the two items if the secondary item does not have an established price. Value is normally measured by how much each item would cost separately, and the total price of the combination cannot be greater than the separate normal prices of each item added together.

For example, if a toothbrush were given away with the purchase of a tube of toothpaste, a combination offer, the toothpaste price could not be raised to cover the cost of the toothbrush. Because the sales promotion is a free combination offer, the combination in this instance must be sold at the going price for the toothpaste and not at an inflated price.

Another example would be if a combination offer of a toothbrush and a tube of toothpaste was made available and the price of the combination could be set to cover the cost of the toothbrush and the toothpaste. But the price of the combination offer could not be higher than the total price of both items if they were sold separately. The combination offer cannot be constructed so that the seller makes more on the offer than if the items were sold separately, as this would be false and misleading. In this instance, if the toothbrush usually sold for 59 cents and this size of toothpaste sold for 29 cents, then the combination offer could not exceed 88 cents.

In the combination offer the price that can be charged depends on how the promotion is offered. It must be remembered that a combination offer on products that are sold separately and have established prices cannot be offered at higher prices, because the price is known too well to the consumer; but the real problem arises when the secondary item is not well known and does not have an established price. Here the consumer could be confused as to the value, and the seller could make an exorbitant profit.

Finally, in the case of premiums and free samples or free

premiums, the sample must be a reasonable facsimile of the product that it represents. If the premium is a self-liquidator, then it must be of a value equal to or greater than the normal price of the premium to the consumer. The practice of making a profit on self-liquidators has been frowned upon by the Federal Trade Commission.

All in all, the legal aspects of consumer sales promotion devices are somewhat vague and inexact. The causes of the vagueness are that the laws are not written to correct each of the actions but to cover the deception in general. Also much of the control comes under the Federal Trade Commission, which issues guides for what can and cannot be done in using certain sales promotion devices, but these guides are also very general. Therefore the laws and regulations are interpretative and lack any real concrete examples.

Notes

1. The interpretation of the Robinson-Patman Act is taken from the section dealing with this subject in Earl W. Kintner, *An Antitrust Primer,* The Macmillan Company, New York, 1964, pp. 73–75.

2. Robert A. Lynn, *Price Policies and Marketing Management,* Richard D. Irwin, Inc., Homewood, Ill., 1967, p. 256.

3. Ronald A. Anderson and Dwight A. Pomeroy, *Business Law,* 4th ed., South-Western Publishing Company, Cincinnati, 1952, p. 954.

4. "Gasoline, Food Outlets' Cash-Gift Promotions Held Illegal in Ohio," *Wall Street Journal,* July 18, 1967, p. 32.

5. Stanley E. Cohen, "Mrs. Peterson Stumps FTC in Plan to Tell Consumers His Odds in Giveaways," *Advertising Age,* Oct. 31, 1966, p. 4.

6. "FTC Gets Tough on 'Cents-off' Practices," *Sales Management,* Nov. 15, 1966, p. 12.

INDEX

INDEX

Sampling, methods of, on package, 47
  ring-and-leave, 44
Sandage, C. H., 97n.
Schlitz Brewing Company,
  Joseph, 5
Schultz, William J., 18n.
Shell Oil, 16
Sherman Antitrust Act, 117, 120
Socioeconomic groups, 94
Sperry and Hutchinson Company (S & H), 6, 84
Sports Illustrated, 58
Stimulants, retail *(see* Direct retail stimulants)
Strategy, 18, 48
  (See also Sales promotion, goals of)
Suburbs, 41, 51
Swanson Company, 62
Sweepstakes *(see* Contests and sweepstakes)

Test of coverage, 122
Texaco, 75
Tidewater Oil, 16
Trade deals, 98, 99, 101, 104, 105
Trading stamps, 83–87
  definition of, 83
  limitations of, 86
  objectives of, 84–85
  operations, 85–86
Trial size, 37
Turnover, 41

Unduplicated coverage, 55
Urban living, 41, 51

Wall Street Journal, 128n.
Webb-Pomerene Act, 117
"Win-a-Check," 16
Wolff, Janet, 64n.

Zacher, Robert V., 33